MENTAL TRAPS

The

OVERTHINKER'S

GUIDE

to a

HAPPIER LIFE

ANDRÉ KUKLA

ANCHOR CANADA

LIBRARY AND ARCHIVES CANADA CATALOGUING IN PUBLICATION

Kukla, André, 1942–
        Mental traps : a field guide to the stupid mistakes that can ruin your life / André Kukla.

ISBN 978-0-385-66250-5

    1. Errors—Psychological aspects.   2. Self-actualization (Psychology) 3. Habit.   I. Title.

BF637.S4K843 2007   158.1   C2007-900297-8

Book design and illustrations: Kelly Hill
Printed and bound in the USA

Published in Canada by
Anchor Canada, a division of
Random House of Canada Limited

Visit Random House of Canada Limited's website:
www.randomhouse.ca

RRD 10 9 8 7 6 5 4 3 2 1

To my mother and father,
Lily and Leo Kukla

CONTENTS

1.

The Nature of Mental Traps . . . 1

2.

Persistence . . . 13

3.

Amplification . . . 27

4.

Fixation . . . 45

5.

Reversion . . . 59

6.

Anticipation . . . 75

7.

Resistance . . . 101

8,

Procrastination . . . 117

9,

Division . . . 135

10,

Acceleration . . . 153

11,

Regulation . . . 167

12,

Formulation . . . 185

13,

Keeping Out of Mental Traps . . . 197

Appendix
The Practice of Thought-Watching . . . 219

the Nature of
Mental Traps

1.

Mental traps are habitual modes of thinking that disturb our ease, take up enormous amounts of our time, and deplete our energy, without accomplishing anything of value for us or for anyone else in return.

The word "value" here, and throughout this book, refers to whatever seems worthwhile to us. This book is not a moral tract. It doesn't take the side of useful work against recreation, or social involvement against self-indulgence. If we're content to watch television all day, then this activity will not be counted here as a waste of time. Watching television has value for us.

The fact remains that we often exhaust ourselves in troublesome pursuits that don't in any way further the actualization of our very own values, whatever they may happen to be. These useless pursuits are the mental traps. Mental traps keep us from enjoying television as readily as they keep us from serious work. They are absolute wastes of time.

Mental traps are identified not by the *content* of our ideas but by their *form*. Any aspect of daily life—household chores, weekend recreation, careers, relationships—may be thought about either productively or unproductively. We fall into the same traps when we wash the dishes as when we contemplate marriage or divorce. It's not the subject of our thinking, but how we deal with the subject, that makes the difference. When we rid ourselves of any one trap, we find that our problems in every department of life are simultaneously eased.

We build unproductive structures of thought on every conceivable timescale. One and the same mental trap may hold us in its sway for a fleeting moment or for a lifetime. And the momentary traps are just as pernicious as the lifelong traps. Because of their brevity, the mere moments of wasted time and energy are especially difficult to grasp and correct. They're over and done with before we're aware of what we're doing. The result is that they're fallen into with monumental frequency. It's doubtful that the average twenty-first-century urban adult is altogether free of them for more than a few minutes at a time. By the end of the day, the cumulative effect of these brief episodes may be an entirely unaccountable exhaustion.

4

The basic idea underlying mental traps was concisely expressed a few thousand years ago:

To everything there is a season, and a time
for every purpose under Heaven.

When we deviate from this profound advice—when we begin at the wrong time, proceed at the wrong pace, quit too soon or too late—we fall short of what we might otherwise accomplish.

Again, there's no attempt here to prescribe the content of our activities. To *everything* there is a season. Both the enjoyment of good food and the scramble up the ladder of success may be legitimate parts of our life. But if we try to advance our career while we're eating dinner, we ruin our digestion—and we can't really do good work as we pass the salt and slurp the soup. Neither of our values is well served. Given the same values, we could make far better use of our time and resources.

Our lapses from doing the best thing at the best time and in the best way fall into recurrent and readily identifiable patterns. These are the mental traps.

—

If mental traps are injurious to us, why do we fall into them? Why don't we simply quit? There are three reasons. First, we're often unaware of what we're thinking. Second, even when we are aware of our thoughts, we often don't recognize their injurious nature. Third, even when we recognize their injurious nature, we often can't quit because of the force of habit.

If the thinking that goes on when we're trapped remains below the level of consciousness, we can't even begin to change it. We can't choose to stop doing what we're not aware of doing in the first place. If we didn't know that we wore clothes, it would never occur to us to take them off, even if we felt too hot. By the same token, when we don't know that we're thinking unproductive thoughts, the option of stopping doesn't present itself.

The idea that we can be unaware of our own thoughts may strike us as paradoxical, for we tend to equate consciousness with thinking itself. But the two are by no means identical processes. We may be exquisitely conscious of the taste of an exotic fruit or the feel of an orgasm without having a thought in our head. And we may be filled to overflowing with an unbroken stream of ideas without noticing a single one. The following mental experiment will convince us of this important point.

When we aren't occupied with any definite business or pleasure, our thoughts often wander from one topic to another on the basis of the flimsiest associations. This experiment can be conducted only when we happen to catch ourselves in the midst of such wanderings. For those who don't fall asleep quickly, the time spent lying awake in bed is especially rich in this material. As soon as we catch ourselves wandering, we can begin a backward reconstruction of the sequence of ideas that led us to where we are. If we were thinking about the beauty of Paris, we may recall that this was preceded by a thought about a friend who has just returned from there. The idea of the friend's return may have come from the recollection that this person owes us money, which may in turn have come from ruminations about our financial difficulties, which may have been elicited by the idea that we would like to buy a new car.

In this experiment, it's essential *not* to decide ahead of time that we *will* reconstruct the next few minutes of thought. We have to wait until we catch ourselves in midstream. When this happens, we're invariably surprised at the twists and turns taken by the stream of our ideas. Without an active reconstruction, we would never have suspected that the thought of Paris had its origin in the desire for a new car! And it's this experience of surprise that proves the point. *We wouldn't be surprised unless we didn't know what we had been thinking.* Our thinking was unconscious. Evidently, the process of thinking no more depends on our continuous attention to it than walking depends on our continuously keeping track of the position of our arms and legs.

Mental traps often remain below the level of awareness in just this way. We fall into them automatically, without making a conscious decision. The first requirement for getting rid of them is to learn the art of detection. This book provides the materials necessary to meet that requirement. It's a naturalist's guide to a certain order of mental flora, outlining the conspicuous characteristics of its various members, replete with illustrative examples. It's a handbook for the identification of mental traps.

Learning to detect and identify the traps is the first step. But detection and identification aren't enough to put an end to them. We also need to be convinced that they're useless and injurious. This isn't always obvious. In fact, mental traps are often mistaken for absolutely essential activities without which life would become chaotic and dangerous. Some traps are even celebrated in famous proverbs. We will not move against them until we're thoroughly convinced that they have no redeeming value.

Every good naturalist's guide contains this sort of practical information. What's the use of learning to identify the amanita mushroom if we're not also told that it's poisonous? In this handbook too, the various aids to the identification of mental traps are supplemented by analyses of their harmful effects.

Having learned to identify the traps and having been convinced that it's to our advantage to be rid of them, we are left with an ordinary case of a bad habit. At this stage, we're like a smoker who has accepted the findings of the surgeon general's report. As every smoker knows, it's only now that the real battle begins. In the battle against mental traps, as in the battle against smoking, resolutions will be made and broken and made again. Some people will succeed in kicking the habit and some will fail. Many will at least be motivated to cut down. The last chapter of this book offers strategic advice for how to conduct this battle against mental traps.

Naturalists have to go to the forest to encounter the objects of their studies. Hunters after mental traps find their prey in the midst of everyday life. It's in the most ordinary affairs—in shopping, balancing the checkbook, keeping appointments, answering the telephone, brushing our teeth, talking to a friend—that we learn most about mental traps. When the stakes are high, we become too fixed on the outcome to maintain an observational attitude toward ourselves. But when the activity is more or less routine, we find the mental leeway to examine what we do and the courage to try a new approach.

When we begin to study ourselves in this way, we reap an unexpected benefit quite aside from the increase in self-knowledge. Ordinary life immediately becomes extraordinary and fascinating. A telephone call in the midst of our work is no longer merely an irritation—it's a prized opportunity to observe the effects of interruptions. Arriving late for a movie gives us a chance

to investigate the nature of small disappointments. Working under a deadline is endlessly rich
in opportunities for self-discovery. Washing the
dishes is an arena in which we may observe the
play of diverse psychological forces—the same
forces, in fact, that contend at the most remarkable junctures of life. Were it not for these little
trials and tribulations, we would be unable to
learn anything about ourselves. So we begin to
welcome trouble as an ally, and to be fascinated
by our reactions to it. And everyday life is transformed into an endless adventure. For what is
adventure if not an attitude toward trouble?

It's time to begin our exploration of the internal landscape. We needn't be in too great a hurry
to change things around. Drastic intervention can
wait until we understand the ecological balance
of this unfamiliar terrain. Meanwhile, let's enjoy
the sights. Even the amanita mushroom has its
beauty.

Persistence

2.

he first trap, *persistence*, is to continue to work on projects that have lost their value. The activity had meaning for us once—or we would never have begun. But the meaning has evaporated before we reach the end. Yet we go on, either because we don't notice the change or out of sheer inertia.

We start a Monopoly game with great enthusiasm and—inevitably—get bored before we reach the end. But instead of quitting, we toil on without pleasure "just to get it over with." There can be no clearer example of a waste of time.

Someone asks us to recall the name of a supporting actor in a B movie of the forties. It's on the tip of our tongue, but we can't quite come up with it. Meanwhile the person who wanted to know has departed from the scene. But her problem doesn't depart with her. It bedevils us all day. Originally our aim was to answer someone's question. But this aim isn't what keeps us going now. Even the other's death wouldn't relieve us of our burden.

We start to watch a television show and soon realize that it's hopelessly dull. Yet we watch it "to the bitter end," complaining all the while about how awful it is.

We foolishly begin to sing "A Hundred Bottles of Beer on the Wall." When we pass the eighty-five-bottle mark, we're already sick of the enterprise. But we don't quit. Instead, we sing faster and faster so that we may sooner come to the end.

In a political discussion, we conceive of a decisive but lengthy refutation of our opponent's view. Halfway through our exposition, he announces that he's convinced. We need say no more. Yet we tediously bring the argument to a superfluous conclusion.

We aren't sufficiently impressed by the sheer peculiarity of actions like these.

What makes these activities mental traps is that they proceed without reference to our needs or interests. It doesn't ordinarily give us pleasure to carry on with them to the bitter end. On the contrary, the too-long Monopoly game, the struggle to remember trivial information, and the awful television show are experienced as irritants. We're impatient to be done with them, and relieved when they finally do come to an end. If there were a pill that could make us forget we were ever asked about the B-movie actor, we would gladly swallow it. Those who espouse the hedonistic view that we always act to maximize our pleasure would be hard put to explain phenomena like these.

Of course, we may persevere for values other than pleasure. We may finish a tedious Monopoly game in order not to disappoint a child. We may watch an awful show to the end because it's our job to write a review. We may sing our way down to the last bottle of beer as an exercise in patience. Joyless perseverance is not always the trap of persistence. But most watchers of awful television shows are not critics, and most singers of "A Hundred Bottles of Beer" are not engaged in spiritual exercises. They're accomplishing nothing, and not enjoying it.

Incredibly, our culture teaches us to regard persistence as a virtue. We boast that once we are set on a certain course, nothing can dissuade us from following it to the end. We teach our children that it's a sign of weakness, even of immorality, to leave anything half-done. It's undeniable that our affairs benefit greatly from the capacity to persevere in the face of adversity. But it's quite another thing to suggest that this capacity should always and indiscriminately be exercised. A useful distinction may be drawn between *persistence* and *perseverance*. We persevere when we steadfastly pursue our aims despite the obstacles that are encountered along the way. But we merely persist if we doggedly carry on in directions that are known to lead to a dead end.

The moral imperative to finish everything we start is deeply ingrained. We find it difficult to abandon even the most transparently vapid enterprises in midstream. The mere act of beginning already binds us to continue to the end, whether or not the original reasons for the activity remain valid. We act as though we were bound by a promise—a promise made to no one but ourselves.

We begin to watch a television show solely for the sake of amusement. But a second motive enters the picture almost immediately: the need to complete what was begun. So long as we remain amused, this need can scarcely be felt. It's a push in the direction we are already traveling. But its effect is noticed as soon as we lose interest in the show. Were amusement the only motive for watching, we would quit immediately. But the secondary motive to finish what was begun, just because it was begun, makes us persist.

Newton's laws stipulate that a moving body will continue to move in the same direction until its inertia is overcome by other forces. It seems that we also obey a law of *mental inertia*. Having begun an activity, we are kept moving in the same psychological direction until we reach the end. As in the case of physical inertia, this impulse may be overcome by other tendencies. Not every Monopoly game is played out to the end. An earthquake, a sudden flood, or a full bladder will put a stop to all but the most stubborn cases of persistence. Even ordinary boredom may be strong enough to make us quit. But we must be more than a little bored, the emergency must be more than a little pressing, our bladder more than a little full. Inertia systematically tips the scale in favor of continuing with the task at hand regardless of the merits of the case. The result is that our decision to quit often comes a little too late.

It takes but a moment's resolve to launch ourselves upon the vastest enterprises. Once we're launched, however, we can't simply cancel our plans with another momentary act of will. We've lost the "off" button.

We sometimes try to justify persistence by saying that we don't wish our investment of time and energy to come to naught. If we quit the game now, our previous efforts to win will have been in vain. This line of thinking explains why an ongoing state of persistence becomes progressively more difficult to terminate. If we've completed only a few moves of a boring game, our investment is so small that we may write it off with little regret. But after several hours of grim and pleasureless play, it seems a shame not to go a little longer and finish up. So much effort will have gone to waste!

Of course this is a spurious argument. The pleasureless hours have *already* gone to waste. They won't be redeemed by finishing up. It's time to cut our losses and run. Paradoxically, our instinct for conservation leads only to more waste.

The absurd reluctance to let go of worthless things may even cause us to embark on activities that have no value right from the start. We may buy objects that are of no use to us because we can't waste the opportunity of a sale, or eat when we aren't hungry so that the food won't have to be thrown out, or cart home junk from other people's attics. This trap is a first cousin to persistence.

Here we're not caught in midstream by the dis-
appearance of a previous value. What we do has
no value from the moment we begin. For the
sake of formal elegance, we may consider it to
be a limiting case of the same trap. In this type of
instantaneous persistence, it's advisable to quit as
soon as we start.

Boring games, awful shows, and sales on
items we can't use possess the happy property of
coming to an end by themselves. Not all activities
are self-terminating, however. A job, a marriage,
or a habit is potentially forever. When an enterprise of indefinite duration loses its value, we
may be plunged into a state of *perpetual persistence*. The mere passage of time will not deliver us
from this trap. We're in a Monopoly game that
never ends.

We may perpetually persist at relationships
that have turned irretrievably sour, jobs that hold
no present satisfaction for us and no hope for the
future, old hobbies that no longer bring us pleasure, daily routines that only burden and restrict
our lives. Often we stay on a fruitless course
simply because we don't think to re-evaluate our
goals. We've lived like this for so long—with
this person, at this job, in this house and this

neighborhood, wearing this style of dress, enacting these dietary and hygienic rituals in this particular order—that it no longer occurs to us that things could be otherwise. Our drab and hateful existence is taken to be an absolute condition imposed on us by fate, like the shape of our head. We may not like it, but there it is. If we stopped to ask ourselves whether we wish to continue along our present course, the answer might be crystal clear. Any amount of insecurity would be preferable to doing *this* for eight hours a day, five days a week, fifty weeks a year, until we die. But we don't always ask ourselves. We complain, but we take the necessity of the status quo for granted. Hence we persist in the very patterns of behavior that sustain it. Since the option of quitting doesn't present itself, the only alternative is to "get it over with," like a tedious Monopoly game. Unfortunately, this tedious game constitutes our whole life.

Our unwillingness to abandon a bad situation may also stem from a belief that the alternatives are even worse. Perhaps we'll starve if we quit our job. Our view of the matter may or may not be correct. In either case, this reason for staying on is not a mental trap. It's the best choice we can make given our understanding of the situation. But we must watch out that we don't use this type of argument to rationalize the sheer force of inertia. Sometimes we simply can't change, although every indication cries out that we should. We feel compelled to stay on the same course just as we're driven to finish the Monopoly game. So long as we remain conscious of our dilemma, there's some hope that we will break out of the deadlock. Once we've neatly rationalized our situation as the best choice of a poor lot, however, it's all over for us.

It's particularly easy to fall into a perpetual case of *negative persistence*. Here we persist in *not* doing something that *would* be rewarding. We never open ourselves up to an intimate relationship because we did so once before with disastrous results. We never eat olives because we tried one twenty years ago and had to spit it out. We never tackle mathematical problems because we were terrible in math at school.

Not doing something is also a project without an end. We are never finished avoiding olives. These habits of omission are therefore liable to persist perpetually. In fact, they are *especially* liable to persist. It's relatively easy to see when we should quit *doing* something, such as eating the same tasteless cereal every morning. We need only consult our experience. But how will we discover that it's time to quit *not* doing something, such as avoiding olives? Perhaps we would enjoy them now if only we tried them. But so long as we negatively persist, there's nothing in our experience to tell us so.

Negative persistence is the mental structure underlying many phobias. Having once had a bad experience in a large crowd, or driving along a mountain road, or speaking before an audience, we avoid the object of our distress forever after. The initial experience may have been due to a unique confluence of factors. Other crowds, other roads, other audiences, or even the same ones on another day may not have affected us at all. But because we avoid them all, we're not in a position to find out. Of course this problem is further compounded by the fact that our expectation of panic tends to act as a self-fulfilling prophecy. But that's another trap.

If we refrain from an activity, how are we ever to know that its value has changed? The only answer is not to give up on anything for all time to come. It's a good idea to cast an occasional glance at what we have excluded from our life because it's too distasteful, painful, or difficult. Unbeknownst to us, our tastes, our courage, our abilities, our luck, or the world itself may have changed. An annual nibble at an olive or an intimate relationship may pay off handsomely in the end.

A̶mplification is the trap of working harder than necessary to achieve our aim, as when we swat a fly with a sledgehammer. The opposite error of doing too little receives far more attention. But too much is also a mistake. There's a certain amount of work appropriate to each of life's tasks. If we do too little, we fall short of the goal. And if we do too much, we squander our resources.

A comparison with persistence will help to define the character of both traps. When we amplify, the end we are working toward remains valuable, but our work doesn't advance us toward it. When we persist, our work may be superbly effective in moving us toward the end, but we have no reason for going there. We persist when we continue to play a game that has become tedious. We amplify when we take too long to move in a game that we still care about.

It's amplificatory to rehearse a speech so often that our words become dull and lifeless, or to spend a hundred dollars to make the projection of our annual expenditures more precise by ten dollars, or to overpack for a trip because we wish to be prepared for the most unlikely contingencies—what if we're invited to a formal ball in the midst of the Papuan jungle? Making more money than can be spent is an amplification that has consumed some lives in their entirety.

The mark of amplification is that the means exceed what is necessary to accomplish the end. Whether we are amplifying therefore depends on what we're trying to accomplish. Making more money than we can spend is a trap if our aim is to be able to buy what we want. But the same activity may be fully in accord with our values if we engage in it for the pleasure of playing the money game. A man's prolonging sexual foreplay longer than strictly necessary to ejaculate doesn't count as amplification—unless his only interest is in reproduction. Even swatting a fly with a sledgehammer may be appropriate if we feel the need to exercise. On the other hand, it's unlikely that we overpack for the sake of exercise or out of a fascination with the packing game. Still, it isn't unheard of.

There are tasks that provide literally endless opportunities for amplification. However much we do in the service of these goals, it's still possible to do more. If we want to be rich, there's always more money to be made. We can always rehearse a speech one more time. If we keep looking, there's always a chance that we'll find a higher-scoring Scrabble word. And when we make a decision, there are always additional factors that may be taken into account. Having compared the academic reputation, athletic prowess, and architectural merits of several universities, we may also essay a guess as to where we're most likely to find romance. Having discussed our options with a dozen people, we can always solicit the opinion of a thirteenth.

Of course there is a law of diminishing returns. Our second million dollars may not make enough difference in our life to be worth the trouble of making it. And our deliberations about schools must eventually reach levels of such minute significance or vast uncertainty that it isn't worth the effort to carry the analysis further. This is the point where amplification begins.

We're sometimes persuaded to go beyond this point by the thought that we can never really be sure that more work will prove to be useless. For all we know, one more minute of looking at the

Scrabble board will reveal a place for our seven-letter word. The thirteenth informant may give us vastly better advice than the previous twelve. But if this line of reasoning is sound after twelve informants, it's equally sound after thirteen. The next bit of effort may indeed be crucial—and so may the next bit after that, and the one after that. By this argument we're led to the conclusion that we should study the Scrabble board forever and consult with every person in the world about our options.

The fallacy of such thinking is that it's a cost-benefit analysis that leaves the cost entirely out of account. To be sure, it's always possible that we may profit from more work. But it's also certain that more work will cost us time and effort that we could choose to spend otherwise. The question is not whether more work on the present activity might benefit us, but *whether it's likelier to benefit us than the same amount of work invested elsewhere*. This is the criterion for when to quit.

The application of this criterion is clearer in some cases than in others. At one extreme are situations where the cost of more work actually exceeds the potential benefit. Suppose we have to make nine different stops on a shopping expedition. Unless we plan a route beforehand, we'll end up needlessly retracing our steps. But if we try to work out the very best route by estimating the time it would take for all 362,880 permutations of nine stops, our calculations will surely take longer than the amount of traveling time saved by the result. This is the most flagrant type of amplification. We don't even need to inquire whether there are more profitable investments for our time. We would do better not to invest at all. This venture is a dead loss.

On the other hand, we can't say precisely when our deliberations about universities turn into amplification. But we should at least know to quit if it finally becomes clear that we could be doing something more valuable. Even then we may be making a mistake. The very next bit of work might indeed have spelled the difference between success and failure. Freedom from mental traps is not omniscience. But we're more likely to go wrong when we are trapped.

Work may be amplified literally to infinity in either of two directions—horizontally or vertically. In *horizontal amplification*, we think of more and more subtasks to perform in the service of achieving our objective—more people to interview, another rehearsal of our speech, another minute to look for a Scrabble word. Each additional subtask advances our cause less than the last. The value of our work never quite gets down to zero, however. Thus we continue to think that we are usefully employed. The problem is that there are other worthy ventures in life besides this Scrabble game.

Vertical amplification is more intriguing. Here the completion of the major task requires the prior completion of a subtask, whose completion in turn requires the prior completion of a sub-subtask, and so on. Wishing to convey our meaning precisely when we speak, we begin with a prefatory qualification designed to allay misunderstanding:

Not that I insist on this myself, but—

In the midst of our qualification, it occurs to us that the qualification may itself be misunderstood. So we launch into a qualification of the qualification:

> Not that I insist on this myself—nor on any
> of the other options, for that matter—but—

Of course, the qualification of the qualification is also liable to certain misconstructions:

> Not that I insist on this myself—nor on any
> of the other options, for that matter—of
> course I do have preferences—but—

In this way we're led backward away from the goal of deciding on a pizza to considerations of the origin of social contracts, the meaning of life, and the definition of "definition."

Or suppose we try to decide whether to buy a modest but affordable cottage or the sumptuous mansion of our dreams. We reason that our choice depends largely on how financially secure we expect our future to be. But we can't know whether our financial future is secure until we know how likely it is that our particular sector of the economy will flourish in the long term. The probability that our sector will flourish depends in turn on energy prices. Energy prices will depend on our foreign policy. Our foreign policy will depend on the results of the next election.

The next election will be decided by attitudes toward gay rights . . .

The result of vertical amplification is a paradoxical movement further and further away from the goal. The more we work, the more there is left to do before we're finished. A bottomless abyss opens up between the beginning and the end.

In its fullest flower, amplification unfolds in both the horizontal and the vertical directions at once. The task calls forth endless subtasks, each of which requires endless sub-subtasks for their completion, and so on. Can such monstrous mental growths really exist? Where else does chronic indecision come from? If indecision were nothing more than finding the alternatives exactly equal, we would simply flip a coin and be done with it. There would be no reason to *abide* in the undecided state. We remain undecided because we don't know whether the alternatives are equal or not. We can't arrive at their values at all. We're lost in endless calculations.

Accumulation is a particularly insidious form of vertical amplification. We fall into this subtle trap when the goal admits of unlimited degrees of realization. Getting pregnant proverbially does not admit of degrees—either we are, or we aren't.

Nor does coming to a decision—having decided, the job is done. But if we aim at wealth, fame, wisdom, power, or virtue, there is no absolute token of attainment. A millionaire is wealthy compared to the average person. But millionaires are more apt to look to multimillionaires for their standard of comparison. The same relativity affects our judgments of wisdom, power, and virtue. If a turnip were elevated to the station of the average man, it would suppose itself to be a god.

But only for a moment. In fact, no amount of power can make us *feel* powerful for very long, nor does any amount of recognition continue to be experienced as great fame. The attainment of any degree of these indefinite goals, rather than signaling an end to our striving, inevitably becomes the occasion for raising our standard of achievement. Every step forward makes the goal move one step back. Thus we can never arrive. Many lives are given up entirely to these fruitless journeys.

The curious phenomenon of *repetition* occurs in amplification, as well as in several other traps. In all cases the outward manifestation is the same. Having finished our work, we proceed to do it all again. When it's a case of amplification, we repeat in order to achieve a greater and greater degree of certainty that the work is indeed complete. After all, it's always possible that we've overlooked something. Even if we recall having done everything, our memory may be mistaken. So we do it all again. But we don't thereby arrive at a state of *absolute* certainty. There's still room for improvement. So we do it a third time . . . Repetition is a horizontally infinite amplification.

We make all our preparations for a trip. We pack, arrange for the feeding of pets and the watering of plants, disconnect the telephone, make sure that the faucets are shut, lock the windows and the doors . . . Everything has been attended to. But perhaps there's something we've overlooked. Perhaps we've forgotten to pack the toothbrushes. So we review our arrangements one by one: toothbrushes, pets, plants, windows, doors . . . But we can as well commit an oversight the second time around as the first. The situation remains essentially unchanged. Thus if we were inclined to review our arrangements before, we're going to be equally inclined to do so now: toothbrushes, pets, plants, windows, doors . . . Again and again we are returned to the same starting point. We drive off to the airport with our thoughts running along the same endless circle: toothbrushes, pets, plants, windows, doors . . . toothbrushes, pets, plants, windows, doors . . .

The rationalization of repetition is that with each time around we diminish the probability of error. Now this is undoubtedly true in some cases. The chance of making an arithmetical error is considerably reduced if we repeat the calculation and obtain the same result a second time. Even so, we have to take the law of diminishing returns into account. Every review of our work adds less to our confidence than the previous one. Whether it's worthwhile to review ten times, once, or not at all evidently depends on the cost of conducting the review in comparison to its ever-diminishing benefit. Before we go over a hundred canceled checks a second time to reconcile an eleven-cent discrepancy in our balance, we might ask ourselves whether we would be willing to reconcile someone *else's* checkbook for the payment of eleven cents. If not, it might be wiser to subtract the sum from our balance and find something more valuable to do.

Moreover, it isn't always true that every repetition diminishes uncertainty, even by a hair's breadth. Often we already *have* the highest degree of certainty that is humanly attainable. In that case, repetition accomplishes nothing at all. For example, if our enterprise involves more than a few steps, it's impossible to perceive all the stages of the work at once. When we turn to selecting the toiletries for our trip, the clothes we've packed are no longer before us. We have to rely on our memory that when we *did* attend to the clothes, we judged that phase of the work to be complete. If now we try to recapture the certainty of immediate perception by reviewing the earlier stage of the work, we simply lose sight of the later stage. The greatest attainable certainty is already reached when we recall that we *once* judged the other stages of the work to be done. We can no longer have the direct evidence of our senses to make this judgment now. But there's nothing to be done about it. No amount of shuttling back and forth between the earlier and the later stages of the work will diminish our residual uncertainty.

Nor will it help to write everything down or to have someone follow us everywhere with a video camera. For what has been written or videotaped can be read or viewed only one item at a time. By the time we get to the last items, the first ones will already be out of mind. We are therefore back to where we started, relying on our recollection that everything seemed to be in order when it was before us. Making a list may help us to achieve this maximum of attainable confidence. But if we have it already and make a list in the hope of arriving closer to the certainty of immediate perception, we fall into a trap. We will find ourselves reading and rereading our list to make certain that everything is on it, just as we would mentally repeat our activities without a list. The trap is the same. Only the medium of expression has been changed.

It's especially common to fall into the trap of repetition when the goal's attainment or non-attainment is difficult to confirm. When we go to the corner store, we feel very little need to retrace our steps in order to establish that we have come to the right place. But if we want to be loved by another, our attainment may not be so clear even after we've gathered all the evidence we can. But if we *have* gathered all the evidence we can, there's nothing more to be done—except to repeat. This is why some spouses ask for the same proofs and declarations of their mates' affection again and again. And a jealous husband may literally retrace his wife's steps again and again in a vain attempt to eliminate every chance of infidelity.

Whatever their need might be, such people don't sufficiently appreciate the sheer *uselessness* of their actions. Sometimes the available evidence is simply inadequate for our purposes. That may be unfortunate. But nothing is accomplished by going over and over the same ground.

In tracking down the various forms of amplification in everyday life, it's sometimes useful to stop what we're doing and ask ourselves whether our work is really necessary in light of our aims. A good time to ask is when we notice that we're working very hard and not getting much done. But, except when the stakes are large, it isn't usually a good idea to try to calculate benefits and costs with mathematical precision. In fact, this activity can easily turn into yet another amplification. It's pointless to engage in prolonged and relentless inquiries into the value of a three-minute task. We would do better to put in the three minutes and be done with it, whether the work is useful or not.

Often we can detect amplifications simply by their feel. As we've seen, many amplified tasks have a literally infinite structure. We are returned again and again to where we started, or one thing invariably leads to another. These labyrinthine patterns of thought make us literally dizzy. We feel as though we were on a merry-go-round or falling into a bottomless pit. Sensations of this kind are a surer guide to the trap of amplification than any cost-benefit analysis.

Fixation

4.

n *fixation*, our progress toward the goal is blocked. We can proceed no further until we receive a telephone call, an authorization, a shipment of materials, a new inspiration. But instead of turning to other affairs, we remain immobilized until we can get going once again on the same project. In short, we wait.

In preparation for an eight o'clock gathering at our house, we've cleaned and tidied up, bathed, dressed, laid out the food and drink. Everything is in readiness. But it's only seven-thirty. Now what do we do until the guests arrive? We *could* use the empty interval of time to take care of small chores that will have to be done sooner or later anyway. Or we could indulge in a small pleasure. But we don't *experience* the time before us as empty. It seems to us that we're already occupied: we're throwing a party. It's true that there's nothing for us to *do* about this enterprise at the moment, but we manage to keep ourselves busy with it all the same. Like windup soldiers that march in place when they bump into a wall, we continue to attend to our project even when it doesn't call for our attention. We busy ourselves with the peculiar round of activities collectively known as "waiting for" the guests to arrive. We visualize their arrival. We wish they were already here. We observe the movements of the hands on the clock, literally marking time until we can swing into action again.

Fixation may be conceived of as a limiting case of amplification. When we amplify, the work left to do accomplishes so little that it isn't worth the effort; yet we go on. When we fixate, there is, at least for the moment, *nothing* left to do. And still we go on. In order to accomplish the apparently impossible task of keeping busy when there's nothing to do, we invent completely useless activities that have *reference* to the goal, although they don't advance us toward it in the least.

It scarcely needs to be pointed out that fixation is a waste of time. Indeed, the colloquial name for fixation is "killing time." This felony is routinely committed when further progress depends on a change of circumstances that we can't ourselves bring about—when we have to wait for the guests to arrive, the checkout line at the grocery store to move, the traffic to unsnarl, the five o'clock whistle or the three o'clock school bell to signal an end to our incarceration.

In circumstances like these, we stare at clocks, count to ourselves, twiddle our thumbs, gaze about randomly without letting ourselves get interested in what we see, complain about our plight, and spend time wishing that the period of waiting were over. These activities sustain the illusion that we're still laboring at the stalled enterprise. Our clock-watching is felt magically to keep time moving, and the force of our complaints and wishes seems to push the checkout line along.

Another way to keep busy when there's nothing to do is by repeating what's already been done. The host waiting for his guests to arrive will double-check and triple-check his preparations. We've already encountered repetition as a form of amplification. The behavior is the same; but it's even more senseless in the context of fixation. When repetition is amplificatory, we at least expect to obtain a greater degree of certainty that the job has been properly done. But the fixated host entertains no doubts about the adequacy of his preparations. He double-checks and triple-checks simply to kill time.

If the repetitions, the wishings, and the complainings begin to run thin, we may be privileged to observe the last refinement of fixation: the state of *suspension*. Having exhausted every device for keeping busy when there's nothing to do, we still don't tear ourselves away. Instead we sit vacantly, benumbed, in a state of mental paralysis. But this vacancy isn't simply an absence of thought. Paradoxically, the suspended mind is both empty of content and fully occupied. We feel the strain of mental exertion. We are busy. Yet if asked to describe what we are doing, we have nothing to say.

When we can't do anything useful to advance our aim, we would do better to forget about it and turn to something else—even if the aim is enormously important and the alternative is just barely worth a glance. Any amount of value is preferable to merely killing time. Until we're in a position to do something constructive about saving the world from a nuclear holocaust, let's have a cup of tea. When we're standing in line, we can observe the other people or enjoy a private fantasy. When we're stuck in traffic, we can do isometric exercises. Periods of enforced waiting are often precious opportunities to indulge in the little pleasures of life for which we can't make a special time in our busy day. Here at last is a chance to take a leisurely bath or an aimless stroll, to throw sticks for a dog, to discuss philosophy with a child, to interpret the shapes of clouds. In fixation, we throw away the gift of an empty moment.

The alternatives to killing time are sometimes limited by the circumstances in which we have to wait. We can't observe the clouds from a windowless waiting room. But one option that's always open to us is to not do anything at all. This at least conserves our energies for the time when we're once again called into action. When there's nothing to do, it's a waste of electricity to keep the mind running. Here at last is a chance to take a break from the incessant mental chattering—the planning, the scheming, the hypothesizing, the evaluating—that modern life seems to require of us.

Of course, not doing anything has to be distinguished from the contentless mental activity of suspension. The latter exhausts us; the former rejuvenates. When the mind is empty, awareness flows effortlessly with the endless changes offered up for our delight by a bounteous universe. Not even a waiting room can shut them out: a stain on the ceiling that may be seen as Cleopatra on her royal barge, an exquisitely ugly wallpaper, a rhythm of hurried footsteps in the hall, the cool leather of the armchair, an inner vision of deities and fabulous beasts . . . The quieter we are, the more we see. When we're suspended, however, we aren't so easily captivated by the passing scene. We're too busy waiting.

The obstacle that makes us fixate may be internal as well as external. We may simply not know what to do next. We try to decide whether a marginal friend should be invited to our party, or whether to eat Chinese food or Italian. We go through whatever procedures are deemed appropriate for decisions of this sort—weighing the benefits against the costs, praying to God for guidance, consulting the entrails of a sheep. And the data prove to be insufficient for settling the issue—the costs exactly counterbalance the benefits, God tells us to decide for ourselves, the entrails are ambiguous. So we complain, we wish, and we repeat. Eventually we fall into a state of suspension. We sit and stare vacantly at the problem, or try to conjure a solution by chanting its name. Chow mein, lasagna. Lasagna, chow mein.

What can we do in a situation like this? If the decision isn't pressing, it should simply be set aside for the time being. Perhaps we'll receive new information that will help us to make up our mind. Perhaps we'll hit upon a new decision-making procedure. Fixating on the problem doesn't invite either of these developments, however. On the contrary, it diminishes the chance of encountering new experiences that may lead us out of our impasse. We're more likely to break through to a solution if we go to bed and dream.

Fixation is senseless even if we can't postpone our deliberations. If we must decide now, it's better to be arbitrary than to sit and stare. If we can't answer a question on an exam, we should guess. Of course the arbitrary decision may be wrong. But abiding in the trap of fixation doesn't decrease this risk at all. So let's stop wasting time and turn to the decision-making procedure that never fails to give a definite result: let's flip a coin.

The most troublesome variety of fixation is undoubtedly *worrying*. To worry is to think unproductively about a potential misfortune that we're powerless to affect. We lose a briefcase on the bus and must wait until morning before we can visit the lost and found. Meanwhile, there's absolutely nothing we can do. Yet our thoughts return to the issue again and again. We "wonder" whether the briefcase will be found. We "hope" that it will be found. We "wish" we hadn't lost it.

We've all heard it a thousand times before: it's no use worrying. Worry does nothing except make us miserable. Unlike so many other traps, this one is widely recognized for what it is—when someone else is the victim. When we are the worriers, however, it doesn't seem nearly so obvious that our activity is pointless and stupid. Without really being aware of it, we have the superstitious feeling that problems will automatically get worse unless we keep them in the forefront of consciousness. Every potential misfortune is seen as a willful adversary who is waiting to stab us as soon as our back is turned. Or perhaps we have to suffer now to placate bloodthirsty gods. In any case, it feels unaccountably *daring* not to worry.

The moments squandered in merely waiting—for the bell to ring, the show to start, the good or the bad news to arrive, the bus to come, the traffic to move, the tedious speech to end— add up to a considerable fraction of life. But quite aside from these transitory episodes, we may also be afflicted with an attitude of *extended fixation* for days or weeks at a time. We cease to do useful work as summer vacation draws near, and we stop enjoying our vacation well before the time of our return. The shadow of the next stage has already fallen on us and we are paralyzed by waiting. It's fixating on Monday that makes it more difficult to enjoy Sunday than Friday night.

The awaited event may even be lost in the mist of the most distant future. While we wait for our ship to come in or our prince to take us away, we remain day after day in the same limbo as the host whose guests have not yet arrived. We don't let ourselves be wholly captivated by anything in the present, because the present doesn't really count. It's no more than a preliminary attraction, something to pass the time until the real show begins. When we have our degree, when the children are grown, when we come into our inheritance, when we retire, when all the onerous chores and duties that keep us from our heart's desire are finally out of the way and everything is settled—then we will begin to live. But there's a long stretch of time to be killed before the golden moment arrives. Meanwhile, we are restless and impatient from morning to night.

While we wait for the real show to begin, the whole of life may pass us by like an insubstantial dream. Our work is never our vocation. Our pleasures are only makeshift. Relationships are just for the time being. Everything we do is a species of thumb twiddling. We may not even know what we're waiting for. In the trap of *empty fixation*, we look forward impatiently to a fate that we can't even name. We don't know what we will be when we grow up, and we never grow up. We're certain only that we haven't yet become who we really are.

But we need never wait to *become* who we are. We are ourselves already, and this is already our life. A prince isn't merely a future king, a little girl isn't just a woman-to-be. Princes, children, students, apprentices, unpublished authors, struggling artists, and junior executives are already something definite and complete. The maximum of life's joys and sorrows is already open to them.

A great irony is hidden in extended fixation. When we finally become what we've waited so long to be, we're liable to be overwhelmed with nostalgia for the good old days. A struggling young actor once gave his wife a bunch of grapes on their anniversary, wishing that they were pearls. Years later, having become a great success, he gave her a string of pearls and wished that they were grapes.

There are no preliminaries to living. It starts now.

I t sometimes becomes clear that our plans have irremediably failed. The game is over and we've lost. The consequences of failure may be dreadful. Nevertheless, there's nothing more to be done. Our moves are exhausted; the deadline is past. If we continue to occupy ourselves with the affair at this point, we fall into the trap of *reversion*.

We study the entertainment section of the newspaper, choose our favorite film, structure the evening so that we're sure to have time to go, take a taxi to the theater—and find that the program has been changed. Or we're held up in traffic and arrive late. Whether we decide to go in anyway or do something altogether different, our thoughts may revert again and again to the unconsummated agenda of seeing that film, or seeing it in its entirety. Naturally, this thinking doesn't change anything. It's a waste of time.

Reversion is the temporal opposite of fixation. In fixation, we work furiously to hasten an immovable future. In reversion, we labor to change the immutable past. We'll see that most of the phenomena of fixation have their mirror image in reversion. There's one important asymmetry, however. When the future, proceeding at its own pace, finally arrives, fixation is at an end. We have what we wished for, although our wishing was superfluous. *But reversion never ends by itself.* We can revert to old grievances and disappointments for the rest of our life, and still the past will remain the same. Our wish to alter it is not merely superfluous—it's forever ungratifiable. The passage of time alone will often cure us of fixation. But we have to get rid of reversion by ourselves. Every reversion is potentially perpetual.

Fixation and reversion share a common strategic problem: how to keep busy at an enterprise when there's nothing to do. In fixation, our make-work consists of active waiting, clock-watching, marking time. This strategy is unsuitable for reversion, since there's nothing to wait for. Everything has already happened. Here the problem of how to keep busy is solved with a remarkably elegant stroke. We invent a ghostly universe of past-conditional events—of might-have-beens and should-have-dones—in which we can work arduously on the no-longer-existing issue for as long as we like. Sparing no effort and no ingenuity, we devise plans for how we might have won the heart of the boy or girl we didn't dare to approach in high school. We prove with Talmudic precision that we should have received an inheritance that went to someone else.

Reversion is the I-should-have disease.

Not all thinking about the past is reversionary. We may have a historian's or a novelist's interest in analyzing what is over and done with. We may review the past in order to avoid making the same mistakes again. We may simply enjoy a recreational fantasy of what might have been, just as we might watch a television show. These cases are easy to distinguish from true reversion. When we're trapped in reversion, our thoughts are still bent on the attainment of the missed goal. We act as though the obstacle to gratification were still before us instead of behind us—as though it could conceivably give way if only we pressed against it long enough and hard enough. Of course we don't consciously believe this. We're guided by an unconscious superstition.

On the other hand, when our interest in the past is historical, novelistic, practical, or recreational, we drop the old goal altogether and take up a new one. Amusing ourselves with a fantasy of high school popularity is a very different matter from striving hopelessly toward the goal of *having been* popular. The first is a tepid pleasure, the second a heartache. The specific ideas that cross our mind may even be the same in both cases: "If I'd asked her to the prom . . . if I hadn't been so fat . . ." But it's only in reversion that these thoughts are marshaled in the service of a futile campaign to grasp at what no longer exists.

In both reversion and fixation, we often give vent to our displeasure. In reversion, we mutter incessantly to our unfortunate theater companions about having arrived late. In fixation, we grumble about arriving early and having to wait. These complaints are entirely useless. But not all complaining is in vain. It's useful to distinguish here between *complaining* and *lamenting*. Complaining is the more general term, referring to any expression of displeasure with the course of events. Lamenting is complaining about what can't be changed. Complaints that aren't mere lamentations may be instrumental in getting things done. This is why there are complaints departments. But there would be no point in having departments of lamentation, where people go to bewail unalterable fates.

Nevertheless there are religious and psychotherapeutic institutions that do a brisk trade in lamentation services. The reason they stay in business is easy to understand. Their customers eventually get tired of lamenting and turn to other affairs, whereupon their increased sense of well-being is attributed to the potency of the lamentation. But they could have felt as well right from the start by skipping the lamenting stage and turning to other affairs immediately. Of course this is difficult for many people to do. The habit of ruminating over past misfortunes is as deeply ingrained as the habit of worrying about the future. Often the attempt to engage in other activities is simply unsuccessful. We try to enjoy the company of the lover we're with, but are haunted by the face of the one we lost. Lamentation isn't a cure for our problem, however. It's the disease.

Reversion is no less a trap after great calamities than after small disappointments. When the thousands who have died in a natural disaster are buried, there are again dishes to wash, letters to write, children to tell stories to, good books to read. It won't help the victims to darken the rest of our days with lamentations. This isn't to say that the dead should be forgotten. Their memory is a precious possession, for we would literally be diminished if they ceased to appear and play their role in our inner life. This realization is the only meaningful commemorative. The dead don't profit from our might-have-beens and should-have-dones, our lamentations, our guilt for having survived. And neither do we.

Still, a life without mental traps is not a life without suffering. Having failed to avert an injury, we feel the pain. And the pain of others hurts us empathetically. The survival of the individual and the social group depends on these mechanisms. But no purpose is served by supplementing the pain of injury with the self-inflicted pain of reversion. When we're laid up with a broken leg, we're uncomfortable enough without plaguing ourselves with thoughts of what we might have done to avoid the accident. It's done.

Guilt is the trap of reverting to a moral failure; *shame* is a very similar reversion to a failure to uphold an image of ourselves. We feel guilty for having caused a child to suffer; we feel shame at being thought of as a person who has caused a child to suffer. Needless to say, these activities are no more helpful than any other form of reversion. The deed is done. Perhaps we should take greater care to avoid such lapses in the future—or perhaps we should change our moral principles or our self-concept. But going on and on about what was done and why we shouldn't have done it is a waste of time.

Guilt and shame are the most troublesome of all reversions, just as worry is the most troublesome fixation. There's a curious difference in our attitudes toward guilt on the one hand, and shame and worry on the other. As we've seen, it's common knowledge that worrying is a trap. It's also become increasingly rare to find propagandists for the value of shame. But guilt still has its fervent spokespersons.

The ancient apology for guilt is that it serves as a deterrent against committing the same offense again. Presumably, guilt works like the pain of touching a fire. Once we've been burned, we won't so readily stick our finger in the flame again. By the same token, the fear of guilt is supposed to motivate us to avoid improper conduct.

But this analogy breaks down at a crucial juncture. Pain follows upon touching fire by itself, independently of our volition. Guilt, however, is something that we do to ourselves. *The aversive feelings associated with guilt are created and sustained by our own intentional guilty thoughts.* If we didn't keep our offense in mind, the feelings would cease to exist. The pain of guilt is therefore more like the pain of a self-inflicted slap in the face than the burn of a fire. We *choose* to do it. But then how can the fear of guilt be a motive for avoiding improper conduct? If the only reason for abstaining from an immoral practice were to escape a self-inflicted slap, we *would not* abstain from it. We would simply choose not to slap ourselves. And if our only motive for abstinence were the fear of guilt, we would choose not to make ourselves guilty. The fear of guilt can't be made to account for the fact that we make ourselves feel guilty, any more than reckless driving can be explained by the fear of accidents.

There's an apparent counterexample to the principle that guilt is a product of our own thinking. In cases of severe depression, people sometimes feel guilty without being able to say what they've done wrong. They know only that they've been unworthy. This *empty guilt* is an exact counterpart in the past to empty fixation in the future. In empty fixation, we wait impatiently for a future glory that we can't even name. In empty guilt, we revert to an unspecifiable past shortcoming. But even here the guilt is sustained by our thoughts. We can't say what we've done wrong, but we think that we must have done *something* wrong. Or we entertain general ideas of our unworthiness. If we didn't think these unspecific thoughts, we wouldn't feel guilty. Of course we may not be aware of our guilty thoughts. The feeling may seem to envelop us despite ourselves, as though it were due to an involuntary glandular secretion. But how can a glandular secretion make a reference to the past? We may feel tired and listless, or agitated and tense without thought. But guilt is inherently an *idea* that brings certain feelings in its train.

The fact remains that when we act immorally, wc feel guilty. But the guilt doesn't simply happen. We do it to ourselves by thinking guilty thoughts. We inflict this suffering on ourselves out of an unexamined, usually unconscious, and entirely mistaken strategy for self-management. We punish ourselves for our immorality with guilt so that we'll be wary of indulging in it again. That is, we treat ourselves as though we were another person whose will could be bent to our own. The essential features of this strategy are the same as if we tried to quit smoking by slapping our face every time we lit a cigarette. The procedure can't possibly yield good results from the point of view of our own values. Either the self-administered punishment inflicts a smaller loss of value than the immorality itself, or it inflicts a greater loss. Let's examine these two cases in turn.

If the punishment is less awful than the immorality of the act, it can't possibly be effective. Presumably, the unhappiness due to committing the offense has proven to be insufficient to make us quit. How then can the smaller misfortune of the punishment have any effect? If a gentle slap could make us quit smoking, then the still more adverse effects of smoking itself could only be more effective. The slap would be superfluous. Similarly, a small dose of guilt can only be easier to bear than the violation of our moral sense. If the immorality of the act doesn't dissuade us, neither will a little bit of guilt.

If, on the other hand, the punishment is more awful than the offense, it may indeed be effective—but we would by definition lose more than we gain. We would quickly stop smoking if each cigarette were followed by excruciating torture. And we would quit our immorality if it were followed by an unbearable dose of guilt. But who would knowingly take a medicine that makes us sicker than the disease? It may be in accord with our values to coerce *others* in this fashion. But we certainly wouldn't want to do it to ourselves. If the self-administered punishment is worse than the offense, we would do better to give in to the lesser evil of the offense.

In sum, either guilt is ineffective, or it makes us lose more than we gain. Either way it's a trap.

Even the most fortunate of lives must leave unactualized an infinite number of possible values. There are people we will never hear of who would have made excellent friends, career options we will never encounter that would have been fulfilling, unknown island paradises. But we don't rue all these omissions from our life. The mere absence of a value isn't yet enough to plunge us into reversion. We must first formulate the missed value as an aspiration that was higher than the actual course of events. We ruminate only about what we once wished for. The non-occurrence of a potential value must be conceived as a palpable *lack* in our reality before we revert to it.

But this distinction between mere non-occurrence and palpable lacking is a piece of mental magic. When an expected visit from a friend doesn't materialize, we think that we've lost something and we are disappointed. If we had not expected him, however, the mere non-occurrence of his visit would have been imperceptible. In reality the two situations are exactly the same: there was no visit. When we remain rooted in what actually *is*, there can be no disappointment, for non-occurrences do not exist. To be sure, they *might* have existed. We *might* have received a visit from a friend. But the friend might have come even if we hadn't expected him. It's not the non-occurrence that makes us unhappy, nor the truth of the past-conditional. What is it then? There might have been fairy godmothers in the world, and multicolored snow, and free lunches. Out of the literally infinite number of non-occurrences that we might have liked, how do we select the ones to bemoan?

The definition of disappointment is radically arbitrary. By fiat, we label certain desirable non-occurrences as things we lack, and ignore an infinite number of other desirable non-occurrences. We may consider ourselves unfortunate when our stock market investments fail to make us any money. Yet at the same time we didn't find any money in the street, no stranger came to us with a gift of money, a wad of bills didn't suddenly materialize in our pocket. All these non-occurrences come to the same thing in the end. But we call only one of them a disappointment.

Since disappointments are both painful and arbitrarily defined, why don't we arbitrarily define them out of existence? The non-visit from a friend and the non-windfall on the stock market have exactly the same status as the non-existence of fairy godmothers. They're games with words. What we call a disappointment is no more than a part of the present conditions under which we must act. Not having made money on the market is the same as not having invested. Losing money is the same as never having had it in the first place. What does it matter how we came to be where we are? Here we are.

Unless we cease to think in the past conditional tense, it's only a matter of time before we are swallowed up by perpetual regret. Our stock of irremediable failures can never be diminished by a single one. It's therefore a mathematical certainty that the opportunities for reversion will increase as the years go by. By the time we're old, we will find ourselves wholly absorbed in the urgent contemplation of an ever more abundant fund of might-have-beens and should-have-dones. If only we'd gone to medical school! If only we'd married! If only we'd lived in California! If only we hadn't wasted so much time in regret!

n all the traps discussed so far, we fall into the error of working too hard. When we persist, we work on a goal that has lost its value; when we amplify, we work harder than necessary to achieve the goal; in fixation, we work on our goal when there's nothing that needs to be done; and in reversion, we work on a goal that's already beyond reach. But working too hard is only one of four cardinal errors. Whatever we undertake, we may do either too much or too little, and we may do it too late or too soon. Only two of these errors are generally recognized in our culture: too little and too late. We seem to make the tacit assumption that the more we work on our projects and the sooner we start, the better will be the outcome. Nothing could be further from the truth.

Anticipation is the trap of starting too soon. It's true that if we start too late, we may not have enough time to finish. But there are also penalties for starting too soon. When we anticipate, we render ourselves liable to *overworking*, *preworking*, and *working in vain*.

———

We *overwork* if we act now when the same result can more easily be attained at a later time. Here is a contrived example that clearly delineates the nature of this trap. Expecting a letter of acceptance or rejection, we compose two replies—one for each possibility. Had we waited until the letter was received, we would have needed to do only half as much work, and the result would have been the same. Hence we overworked. In this case the overwork is so transparent that only the most severely trapped would engage in it. But many of us would be unable to resist giving an occasional thought to each reply in the course of the day. Half of these thoughts are destined to prove useless.

Of course the results are not always the same if we delay. Later on, there may not be enough time to finish the job properly. It's not a trap to act now if a later start would jeopardize the outcome. But much of what we do from day to day can just as well be done at another time. We can just as well mail a letter on Monday morning as on Sunday if there's no weekend postal service. The results would be exactly the same. In that case, the optimal time to act is when this invariant result may be obtained for the least cost in time, energy, and resources. If the cost is the same throughout a period of time, then any time during that period is as good as another for getting the job done. But it often happens that some moments are more opportune for action than others. If we expect to pass a mailbox on our way to work on Monday, for example, it would be anticipatory to make a special trip to the mailbox on Sunday. There's nothing to be gained from the earlier start that might offset the extra work. Similarly, there would ordinarily be no advantage to composing a reply—or even to thinking about a reply—to an expected letter before receiving it rather than afterward. Therefore we should wait until the job simplifies itself.

This analysis doesn't apply to work that's valued for its own sake. If we mail our letter on Sunday because we want to take a walk on a beautiful day, our time has not been wasted, even if we pass by the same spot again on Monday morning. We're glad to have this little excuse to go out. And doing what we like is never a trap.

Generally speaking, work simplifies itself with the passage of time. Delay permits new information to arrive that may save us trouble. Before we commit ourselves to a certain approach, a better one may come into view. Dead ends may be revealed before we butt our heads against them. We may receive a new tool that facilitates the work. Above all, as families of possibilities coalesce into single realities, there's a steady diminution in the number of contingencies that need to be taken into account. In the place of two possible letters to respond to, we have only one real letter. Instead of ten vocational options that are compatible with what we know of our interests and abilities when we're in the sixth grade, there are only two to choose from when we finish high school. Work streamlines itself over time.

This doesn't mean that we should leave everything to the last minute. If we want to travel to the Orient, we can't delay our preparations until the day of departure. There's simply too much to be done. We have to obtain our passports, visas, vaccination certificates, and traveler's checks; our employers have to be forewarned; the cat must be assisted in finding temporary accommodations. It's true that we may later discover easier ways in which some of these tasks might have been accomplished. Unless we take this risk, however, we have no chance of going at all. But if a piece of work *can* be delayed without endangering the chance of its timely completion, then it *should* be delayed. For we lose nothing and gain the advantage of basing our actions on the latest and best information.

Anticipatory overworking is closely related to the phenomenon of amplification. The difference lies in the temporal arrangement of certain events. When we overwork because of anticipation, the same job can be done with less effort if only we wait for a more propitious moment. When we amplify, the same job can be done more easily right now.

Anticipation may lead to *preworking* if there's a chance that our work will be undone by changing circumstances. After we prematurely compose replies to both an acceptance and a rejection, an unforeseen third option materializes: a request for more information. Now we have not merely worked harder than necessary. In this case, our work has come to nothing. We have to begin again from scratch. We might as well have watched TV. What we've done is no more than a useless preliminary to the real job. It was *prework*.

To be sure, we can never make ourselves entirely safe from the undoing of our work by changing circumstances. We engage in exhaustive investigations into the relative merits of Florida and Arizona as retirement homes, and the character of these places changes so drastically in a few years' time that all our calculations are rendered obsolete. No matter how late we act, the Universe may still pull the rug out from under our feet at the last minute. But it's pointless to increase this risk without any hope of compensation. Eventually we must act or suffer the penalty of too-long delay. But *so long as the work can be postponed without penalty, it should be postponed.* For by letting the Universe unfold more of its plan before we act, we diminish the chance that our work will be undone.

A peculiar and extreme type of preworking occurs in *existential anticipation.* We fall into this trap when we make judgments about the nature or quality of life taken as a whole. If we want life to be happy enough or meaningful enough to meet some standard that we've set for it, our goal can be neither definitely met nor definitely missed until life itself has come to an end. Our fate may have been dismal until now; but tomorrow may tell a different story. And a present sense of satisfaction may be taken away from us overnight. "Call no man happy until he is dead," goes an ancient Greek proverb. The final judgment on the quality of our life can't be made in the midst of life itself. Hence it can never be made. Yet we anticipate it. Here is a flagrant example of tackling a problem before all the information is in.

Since our existential judgments are perpetually liable to being undone, it's always too soon to make them. If these perpetually premature assessments are favorable, we only waste some time in useless calculations. But if they're unfavorable, the result can be devastating. Premature negative evaluations of the whole of life are the central feature of chronic depression. In the extreme, they lead to the most anticipatory of all acts: suicide. The suicide looks down the corridor of time to its very end and finds nothing there to make life worth living. What he overlooks is that his information may change. Even if his despair stems from an existential doubt as to the very purpose of human existence, it's possible that this doubt will be resolved in an unimagined way tomorrow, next year, or twenty years from now. But the suicide decides now that this will never happen. In order to pass such a judgment on the whole of his life and its possibilities, he has to view it from a vantage point beyond his own death. Thus he arrives at the final stage of getting ahead of oneself.

Questions about the nature of life taken as a whole are always premature, because we're never finished with living. This doesn't mean that we must always refrain from asking them. They are, after all, fascinating topics for analysis and conjecture. But it's always too soon to settle on an answer.

The third penalty for anticipation is to have *worked in vain* because the value of the goal was lost before we reached it. We purchase theater tickets a week in advance even though the theater has been half empty for every performance. And then we're called out of town on the appointed day, or we fall ill, or read a review so devastating that we lose all desire to attend. Now we're stuck with worthless tickets. In this instance, it's neither a matter of having worked harder than necessary to achieve the goal nor a case of needing to do the work over again in order to resecure the goal. What was secured remains in our possession. But its value is lost. There was no need to do anything in the first place. We have worked in vain. If every performance had been sold out, we would have had to take our chances or give up the idea of going right from the start. As it was, we would have risked nothing by delaying our purchase until the last minute. It isn't having worked in vain by itself that makes our action anticipatory. It's having increased the risk of working in vain for no purpose.

We often end up having worked in vain because our problems take care of themselves. Having considered what to say to an inattentive waiter if he doesn't come to our table in five minutes, we find him before us forthwith, all smiles and apologies. Having struggled for years to make ourselves financially independent, we suddenly inherit a fortune. Our considerations and our struggles have been in vain. Like the risk of finding our work undone, we can never entirely eliminate the possibility that the goal will lose its value before we arrive at it. But again, it's pointless to increase this risk unnecessarily. It costs us nothing to ignore an inattentive waiter until we're actually ready to confront him. By doing our work five minutes ahead of time, we fail to take advantage of the possibility that the problem will disappear without our having to lift a finger. On the other hand, it's perilous to laze about in the hope of receiving a dubious inheritance. If the waiter persists in overlooking us, we're none the worse for having waited until the last moment before dealing with the situation. But we're in deep trouble if the inheritance that we counted on doesn't come our way.

Working in vain is closely related to the trap of persistence. As with overworking and amplification, the difference is temporal. When we persist, we work toward a goal that has already lost its value. When we work in vain, we strive toward a goal that will lose its value before we acquire it. We can never know that we are working in vain until after the fact. The trap is to increase the probability of this event for no purpose.

Certain circumstances seem to invite trapped thinking of more than one sort. One of these occurs when we face a danger that we're powerless to avert. In this situation, we may uselessly worry about our looming misfortune, in which case we fall into the trap of fixation. We may also commit a form of anticipation that causes us to work in vain. In *pre-resignation*, we work on our thoughts and feelings in such a way that we're able to accept the feared event with equanimity.

Threatened by a visit from a tiresome relative, we comfort ourselves with the thought that the evening will soon be over, that tomorrow is another day, that suffering builds character. In short, we resign ourselves to our fate—*before* it overtakes us.

Now pre-resignation is not quite so certainly useless as mere worrying. If the worst does come to pass, we will feel better for having resigned ourselves. But the worst may not come to pass— our relative may come down with the flu—and then we will have made ourselves gloomy for nothing. Our work will have been in vain.

Whether such work is a trap depends, as with all activities geared toward a future end, on whether it can be postponed without penalty. It may be that the impending calamity will leave us in such an enfeebled state that we'll no longer have the inner resources to accept our fate. In that case, we have to assess the relative advantage of resignation before the fact against the possibility of having worked in vain. But it's usually just as easy to resign ourselves after the fact as before. When our relative is firmly installed in our living room, cocktail in hand, we can excuse ourselves for a moment, go into the bedroom, and make our peace as well as we can. Certainly, if we make a habit of always preparing ourselves for the worst, we'll be working in vain far more often than we need. There's usually time enough to accept our fate when it finally overtakes us. Instead of making ourselves perpetually gloomy by always assuming the worst, we would do better to make no assumptions at all and simply continue to live our life. If the worst happens, then we can see how we'll get through it.

Anticipation has a major characteristic in common with the trap of fixation. In both traps, we needlessly concern ourselves with the future. The difference is that in fixation we simply dwell on the future without attempting to do anything constructive about it. In anticipation, our activity is intended to be constructive; but it's premature and therefore liable to overworking, preworking, and working in vain. If we worry that our missing wallet won't turn up at the lost and found, we are fixating. If we make plans to replace our lost driver's license and library card before getting to the lost and found, we're anticipating. Unlike mere worrying, these plans may prove to be useful. But we would do better to postpone their consideration until we knew whether they were necessary. As we saw in the previous section, anticipation is not quite so senseless as worrying and other forms of fixation, since there's at least a chance that anticipatory work will turn out to be useful.

A not-quite-so-senseless anticipation may lay the groundwork for an irretrievably senseless fixation, however. Having begun too soon, we may run out of things to do before the project can be brought to completion. And then we're tempted simply to sit and wait. We start our party preparations too early in the day and finish several hours before the guests are due to arrive—and then we fixate on their arrival. Had we not anticipated, we wouldn't have given ourselves an *opportunity* to fixate.

The greater the amount of time by which we anticipate, the greater the opportunity for subsequent fixation. If we pack for a trip a week too soon, we run the risk of giving up the week to useless musings about the forthcoming venture. It's as if we had already departed. And if we pack two weeks too soon, we take our mental leave two weeks before our body can follow.

At the other temporal extreme of the same phenomenon are miniature episodes wherein we anticipate by a few moments and then fixate for a few moments until the tide of events once again catches up with us. We get up from our seat on the bus before it's necessary—and stand a while by the door. We take out our house key when we're still a block away from the front door—and hold it stuck out before us, ready for action, as we walk down the street. More than one person has been seen to stand at the door of a bus with his keys in hand, looking for all the world as though he planned to unlock the bus to let himself out.

These momentary quirks are not very important in themselves. But they betoken a more general habit of mind that seriously interferes with optimal functioning. The person who takes out her keys too soon is the same one who arrives at the airport too early and sits. Instead of making her actions timely and suited to the circumstances, she follows a rigid pattern of beginning as soon as the task is formulated, doing as much as can be done at this early date, and then waiting, immobilized, until she can continue again. We would expect such mechanical behavior from a simple robot that was built for no other purpose than to turn keys in locks or travel to and from airports. A device of this kind might as well go to the airport right away and turn itself off until the next run. It has nothing else to do.

We're never so prone to anticipation as when we draw up schedules and plans for the future. It's true that we often need to plan what to do at a later time. But planning, like every other form of work, may also be premature. Plans that are made too soon are overwork because they take possibilities into account that would eliminate themselves in time. They're likely to be reduced to prework by changing circumstances that force us to revise our expectations. And they're liable to prove completely unnecessary, in which case the work of planning will have been in vain. The longer we wait before formulating our plans, the less likely we are to suffer these fates.

Of course we can't postpone indefinitely. As with all other forms of work, there comes a time when further delay would be injurious to our cause. In the case of plans, this point can be precisely specified. The time to lay our plans for the future is when they have a bearing on what we are to do *now*. If the dentist's receptionist asks us when we can come in for a checkup, we must immediately make a plan because the receptionist needs an answer *now*. If we contemplate an escape to the golf course, we may have to make a schedule for the rest of the week in order to see whether we can afford to take the day off *now*. What we do now may even depend on our plans for the distant future. We wouldn't apply to medical school *now* unless we had some intention of becoming a doctor in several years' time.

But plans that have no effect on our present activity are anticipatory. By definition, we have no need of them as yet. If we'll be eating dinner for the next half hour, it makes no difference *now* whether we plan to catch up on our work afterward or amuse ourselves. In either case, we're going to be eating this soup, this entrée, and then this dessert. The decision can wait until after dinner. Therefore it *should* wait. After dinner, we may be apprised of an unexpected and wonderful recreational opportunity. And then our plans for working will have been made in vain.

Of all the circumstances in life, the time we least need a plan for the future is when we're already occupied with a valuable activity. So long as the task at hand is clearly necessary or desirable, planning can be postponed without penalty until we're finished. It's enough to know that the present moment is well spent in doing *this*. The future can wait until *this* is over. There's nothing we can do about it now anyway. We're already occupied.

Yet the commonest of all mental traps is to decide what to do next before we're finished with the task at hand. Driving home from work, we decide what to do about dinner. During dinner, we plan the evening's television viewing. Watching television, we organize the next morning's work. At work, we anticipate lunch. At lunch, we cast our thoughts toward the business of the afternoon. In the afternoon, we think about going home . . . This curious habit may be called *one-step anticipation*.

Evidently, we suffer from the delusion that we always need to know what's going to happen next. Without a clear vision of what lies ahead, we feel like a person stumbling in the dark, who may fall over a precipice at any moment. But the analogy is inapt. When we're already engaged in a valuable activity, it doesn't matter that the next step is hidden in darkness because *we aren't going anywhere*. Things are fine right where we are. The need to know what happens next at all times is like a primitive fear of the night that makes us insist that the ground before us be illuminated even when we have no plans to leave the cave. There's time enough to look for precipices when we're ready to step out.

One-step anticipation has consequences that are even more adverse than the usual penalties for anticipation. If we always try to anticipate what happens next, we can never give our undivided attention to the task at hand. The result is that we can never perform the task at hand with maximal efficiency. Immersed in deliberations about our dinner while we're driving, we fail to see the car that suddenly cuts in front of us. And if the present activity is engaged in for the sake of pleasure, our enjoyment is dimmed by the intrusion of the future. Planning the evening's work at the dinner table, we don't notice the taste of our food.

Because their attention is always divided, chronic one-steppers can never function at peak efficiency or experience the higher reaches of delight. This drastic diminution of life is independent of how much of the future they anticipate at a time. There are people who remain perpetually ahead of themselves by only a moment, always casting a sideward glance at the next instant to see what will be happening there. These people might as well be a thousand years away. They're never fully *here*, never just doing *this*. Hence they're never fully alive.

Divided attention is a trap in its own right which may be fallen into without anticipating. Its origin and consequences will be discussed more fully in a later chapter.

The habit of anticipation often passes for a virtue in our culture. We've already met with this curious enthronement of mental inefficiency in our discussion of persistence, and we'll see it again. According to Benjamin Franklin, it's imperative that we anticipate everything that can possibly be anticipated. "Don't put off until tomorrow what you can do today," urges this mad apologist for the trapped state of mind. If we try to live by this hard saying, we will lead a hellish existence. Having done everything that needs to be done today, we can't yet afford the luxury of a leisurely bath, a walk in the park, or a friendly conversation. First we have to take care of tomorrow's business. It's true that we can't yet wash tomorrow's dishes. But the *decision* to wash them tomorrow can be taken today. Hence, if nothing that's currently doable may be postponed, it *must* be taken today. By the same argument, we are right now required to draw up a complete plan of action for tomorrow. Nor can we rest after that. For by Franklin's dictum, the business of the day after tomorrow really should be settled tomorrow; and if it's tomorrow's business, we really should get to it today. The implication of this dismal counsel is clear: we're required to work out a complete scenario for the rest of our life—right now. Needless to say, the more we get ahead of ourselves in this way, the more we overwork, prework, and work in vain.

The structure of thought recommended by Franklin is reminiscent of the vertically infinite amplifications discussed in an earlier chapter: one thing leads to another without end. The perfectly Franklinian life is one vast *vertical anticipation*. No matter how much of the future we've already anticipated, there's always the problem of what happens after that. Having mapped out our career plans for the next twenty years, we have the twenty-first year to think about, and then the twenty-second. Our work is literally never done. The leisurely bath will never come.

There are people who actually live in this condition of endless vertical anticipation. These are the type A personalities that we've read about, who die of stress long before their well-laid plans have run their course. Short of a coronary, the worst thing that can happen to them is complete success, in which case their lives consist of one prefigured scenario after another, each one bereft of spontaneity and the fascination of the unforeseen. They've written the book, and now they plan to spend the rest of their lives reading it.

Anticipation may also be infinite in the horizontal direction. Just as Franklin's vertical anticipator delves further and further into the future, the victim of *horizontal anticipation* prepares himself for more and more possibilities at a single point in time. Anticipating a letter of reprimand, he works out the outlines of an indignant defense. Then the thought occurs to him: what if the anticipated letter takes a conciliatory tone? He had best prepare an alternative version of his reply suited to this eventuality. But what if the letter is whimsical? condescending? whimsical and condescending? whimsical and conciliatory? So he works on six different replies, to make certain that every eventuality is covered. But what if the letter is impersonal and matter-of-fact . . .

Like his vertical cousin, the horizontal anticipator wishes to make certain that he isn't caught by surprise. But he adopts a different battle plan. The vertical anticipator tries to settle what will happen for all time to come; the horizontal anticipator tries to settle what will happen at a particular point of time under all possible circumstances. Both jobs are literally endless. Just as there's no end of time to account for, so also is there no limit to the possibilities for any single point of time. What if we break a leg and can't go to the store? We had best stock up on groceries now. What if the power fails and all the food in our freezer is spoiled? We had best get a generator. What if an oil embargo makes it impossible to obtain fuel for our generator? Perhaps a windmill on the roof . . . Horizontal anticipation is the what-if disease.

The characteristic experience of anticipation is a feeling of being hounded and pushed from behind. As soon as a possible avenue of movement is opened up, we're catapulted along it by a heavy hand at our back. We may not tarry for a moment. It's as though the mere existence of a path made the journey immediately mandatory.

But the fact that something needs doing does not necessarily mean that it needs to be done right now. Even the most important task in the world can be utterly ignored until its time has come. In time, we may be called upon to make momentous decisions, perform heroic feats, lay down our lives. That time may only be a moment away. But until it comes, there's only this night sky to admire, this cup to rinse. Everything else is a trap.

Resistance

7.

There are times when we're called upon to change our course of action even though we are already usefully or pleasantly occupied. The fire alarm rings just as we get to the most exciting part of our book. We hear of an incredibly opportune one-day sale just as we settle down to an afternoon's sunbathing. We spill our coffee all over the papers we were working on. The time has come to redirect our attention. If, at this juncture, we try to hold on to our old course, we fall into the trap of *resistance*.

We're grading 150 long and terrible essays on the administration of President James Buchanan. At the same time, we have to get to the store before it closes for an indispensable item. Without this particular object, we will be in serious trouble before the night is out. Closing time approaches as we draw near the end of our work. The structure of circumstances calls for our going to the store now, before it's too late, and finishing the essays when we come back. One task can wait; the other can't. But we have only five essays left.

It would be such a relief to have the whole business over with and out of mind. We rush through two or three essays more, doing a terrible job, and finally see that we simply must break off. We make a desperate rush to the store. But it's too late. We've resisted change, and now we have to pay the penalty.

There's a close affinity between resistance and the trap of persistence. In both cases, we continue with what we're already doing when it would be better to quit. In persistence, we ought to quit because the present activity has lost its value for us. In resistance, the present task does not lose its value; but we ought to quit anyway because something else more important or more pressing has come up. We persist if we continue to play a game that has become tedious. We resist if we continue to play when there's a fire in the kitchen—even if the game remains interesting.

Both these traps are often set for us by our own mental inertia. Having begun something, we feel impelled to bring it to a conclusion even if its value is lost or exceeded by another alternative. This tendency to stay on the same track can be overcome if the new alternative is sufficiently potent. Fires, floods, and air attacks will bring most people's ongoing projects to a halt. But the inertia of the old task biases our judgment of the optimal time to switch. The result is that we change over to the new course too slowly. When we finally stop grading and run to the store, it's already too late.

Resistance is the let-me-just disease.

There are three conditions under which we should abandon the past and turn to a new future: (1) when delaying our entry into the new diminishes our fortune, (2) when delay causes us to miss a potential increment in our fortune, and (3) when the change to the new is in any case inevitable—that is, when we are visited by *emergencies*, *opportunities*, and *interruptions*.

First, we should drop the task at hand when we're faced with an *emergency*. The essence of an emergency is that if we don't act immediately, we will suffer a penalty for the delay. It makes no difference that the present task is enormously important or that the emergency is very small. What's at issue is only the effect of delay. It's time to stop working on our symphony when the coffee begins to boil. The world can wait a moment longer for our symphony without suffering measurable harm. But the coffee won't wait.

Of course, the task at hand may also be urgent. In that case it is itself an emergency, and we have to decide which of the two can least sustain a delay. It would be unwise to occupy ourselves with boiling coffee when we're struggling with a masked gunman in the living room. The decision to stay on the same track isn't always due to resistance. But if the old activity can be delayed without penalty and the new one can't, it's a trap not to switch.

Second, we should drop the task at hand when *opportunity* comes knocking. In a frenzy of determination, we finally set out to wash all the windows in the house. Halfway through the job, we're invited to an impromptu get-together with our friends. There's no particular reason why the windows should be finished today rather than tomorrow or next week. But the get-together is only today. It's an opportunity. In this instance we have a lot to gain and nothing to lose by changing course. If we opt to finish the windows today, simply because they were begun, we forgo a pleasure for no purpose.

Naturally, freedom from resistance is not a guarantee that opportunities will never again be missed. We may have to decline a sudden and attractive invitation if it will cost us our job to accept. But it's pointless to let opportunity slip away when the present task can be postponed without cost.

We're not likely to forgo opportunities that are very large and obvious. But our reluctance to change course often causes us to miss little pleasures. We won't stop to look at a sunset until we've finished our work—and then it's too late. Even when the opportunity *is* large and obvious, we don't make a transition to it without wasteful effort. We have to tear ourselves away from our half-finished accounts to leave for the rendezvous of our dreams.

It's curious that we should experience any difficulty at all in harvesting an obvious benefit. Our reluctance to face the unpleasantness of an emergency is understandable enough. But mere aversion to unpleasantness can't explain our hesitation in the face of opportunity. It seems that we're unconditionally averse to change itself, whether it's for the worse or for the better. But this is only another way of saying that we suffer from mental inertia.

Third, we should drop the task at hand when we're visited by an imperative *interruption*. The doorbell rings just as we sit down to watch the evening news. We know that a change of course is inevitable. We surely *will* answer the door. We don't seriously consider rejecting the new course. And yet we resist it. We glare at the door and heap maledictions upon it. We delay entering into our new condition even though we can no longer abide in the old. All of this is wasted time and energy.

This isn't to suggest that we should, like a leaf in the wind, accede to every external demand for our attention. The traveling salesman does not always require a full hearing. What matters is the *irresistibility* of the demand. Like everything else, irresistibility is relative to the observer. We can always elect not to answer doorbells and telephones, toss out talkative bores, stay in the race with a broken leg, ignore the cries of a drowning child. But if, for whatever reason, we know that we will not repudiate a call to the new, we might as well stop what we're doing without a fuss. It's irrelevant that our work is enormously important or that the interruption is trivial. If we surely *will* be interrupted, we might as well make the transition gracefully. It's pointless to struggle without a hope of victory.

Resistance to interruptions is the easiest of all mental traps to detect in everyday life. We're always acutely aware of interruptions when they occur, for otherwise they would fail to interrupt us. Thus the occasions upon which we are liable to resist them are clearly signaled beforehand. This makes every interruption into an especially valuable opportunity to practice the skill of not getting trapped. The ring of the doorbell at news-time and the alighting of a talkative bore in the middle of our work provide us with indispensable first exercises in self-improvement. If we remember this beneficial side of interruptions, we will greet them with an openness that already precludes resistance.

The occasions for resistance are greatly increased by certain forms of prior anticipation. When we fall prey to one-step anticipation and needlessly decide what we will be doing next, our decisions are often undone by unexpected circumstances. Having resolved to spend the evening with a book, we're descended upon by the proverbial bore. The work that went into making the decision was in vain. Nevertheless, a decision was made. We *were* to have read a book. Hence the bore is not only unexpected and unpleasant—he's also an interruption. Even if we haven't yet begun to read, we have to tear ourselves away from the *idea* of reading this evening. Had we made no plans for the evening, the arrival of the bore would still have been unfortunate. But we would be spared the trouble of canceling a commitment that we made to ourselves. Hence there are at least two reasons for not making plans unless they fulfill a definite need: (1) we waste the time it takes to make them, and then (2) they cause us to resist unexpected turns of fate.

The champion among makers of useless plans is the vertical anticipator, who strives to work out what he will be doing for the rest of his life. We've already seen that such monumental overplanning is continually being rendered obsolete by unexpected developments. In addition, vertical anticipation engenders continual resistance to the new. When we have a plan for every moment of every day, no person or process in the world can ever take the initiative toward us without our construing it as an interruption. The more specific our plans, the more passive and mechanical we require the world outside ourselves to be. Having written the script for our conversation with a potential date, we require him or her to deliver the proper lines at the proper time, like a phonograph record. If the opening joke is met with a solemn reply, we're lost.

When we carry around a scenario for the rest of our life, we're always busy tearing ourselves away from it.

Resistance in its turn fosters fixation, that is, waiting around until we can resume a blocked activity. One of the reasons we don't take up something new in these circumstances is that the resumption of the old activity may come upon us suddenly and interrupt our new beginning. If we start to read an interesting article while waiting for our guests, they may arrive before we've finished, and then we'll have to tear ourselves away. By remaining on the same course now—by fixating on the guests' arrival—we avoid the strain of changing back to it in the future.

But the change needn't be strenuous. We need only put down the article and go to the door. So long as we don't uselessly resist change, we are none the worse for having begun something that can't be finished right away. Half an interesting article is still better than twiddling our thumbs.

In this situation, the fear of a future bout of resistance leads to a present fixation. In the previous section, we saw that resistance was itself encouraged by anticipation. Causal connections of this kind are widespread among mental traps. One trap always seems to lead to another, and the second to a third. Conversely, the elimination of one trap generally helps us to combat several others. We will encounter more of these inter-connections in future chapters.

In many ways, resistance is the very opposite of anticipation. The occasion for either trap is a choice between perpetuating the past and moving into a new future. There's no generally valid solu-tion to this conflict between the two temporal kingdoms. If we barrel into the future too soon, we are anticipating. If we hold back and stay too long with the past, we resist. Anticipating our departure on a trip, we arrive at the airport too soon and must sit and wait. Resisting our depar-ture because we want to finish tidying up before we leave, we arrive too late and miss our flight. The course of events proceeds at its own pace. Whether we get ahead of the Universe or lag behind, we stumble and fall.

We've already seen that these contrary impulses—anticipation and resistance—often coexist in a single individual. We *resist* every deviation from our *anticipated* scenario for the future. There's something of a paradox here. How can one and the same breast harbor both the tendency to delve too soon into the future and the inclination to cling too long to the past? In fact, these impulses are both aimed at the same effect: the eradication of the unexpected. In anticipation, we banish the unexpected by prematurely settling the course of future events. In resistance, we ward off the unknown future altogether by perpetuating the familiar conditions of the past. Evidently, we operate under the assumption that our control over the reins of destiny should be as tight as possible. The same idea leads, on a societal level, to our indiscriminate appetite for central planning and technological development.

A moment's reflection is enough to see that the validity of this assumption can't be taken for granted. Our life isn't always more fortunate when everything proceeds according to plan. Some surprises turn out well. Resentfully dragging ourselves away from the evening news, we have a delightful evening with an old friend. Our clamber up the ladder of success is brought to a halt by illness, and we find the mental space to review our life and emerge with deeper values. Alternatively, our clamber up the ladder of success proceeds exactly as planned; and we wake up one day to find our children grown before we ever had a chance to play with them. If only their interruptions of our important work had been more effective!

The forces that shape our destiny are infinitely complex. Our plans and decisions are therefore always based on radically incomplete information. Nevertheless, we're often required to make plans. But there's no advantage to making an indiscriminate habit of it, as though proceeding according to plan were an intrinsic good. If the Universe should pull the reins from our hand by visiting us with the unexpected, there's no immediate cause for sorrow. The track record of the Universe is at least as good as our own. A life in which we are always having to react to unforeseen developments is not necessarily less happy or less creative than a life of total self-direction. Even if both lives resulted in equivalent outcomes, the former would have the advantage of sparing us the burden of deciding. With the Universe at the reins, we can relax and enjoy the ride.

The assumption that things always go better when we consciously determine their course finds its quintessential expression in the enthusiasm for biofeedback. How delighted we are at the prospect of controlling our gastric secretions by an act of will! We don't question whether we can do a better job of it than our autonomic nervous system. But what's the basis for this confidence? Has willful direction been so remarkably successful in the rest of our life that we're ready to entrust our stomach to it?

In reality, of course, this striving to extend our control to the furthermost reaches of space and the innermost recesses of our own bodies stems not from confidence in our abilities so much as from a fear of the unexpected. But the unexpected is neither good nor bad. It's another dimension of life entirely. Its elimination may be likened to the extinction of a species or the abolition of the experience of color. If we succeed in scrubbing the world clean of surprise, we will be left with a fragment of our former life.

It often happens that, having unequivocally decided to do something, we nevertheless experience a great deal of difficulty in getting started. The mind simply refuses to get down to business. In preparation for writing a letter, we order up all the papers on our desk. Then we order up all the papers *in* the desk, straighten a picture on the wall, do some calisthenics . . . In short we seek out any small occupation that can take the place of turning to our appointed task. This is the mental trap of *procrastination*. We may or may not get the upper hand over our procrastinative tendency. But even when we do, it takes the usual trap's toll of squandered time and energy.

Some of our procrastinations last for only a moment. Having already decided to run into a burning house and save a child, we still hesitate before entering the flames. Except in the most extraordinary circumstances, these brief fits of procrastination have little effect on the course of our life. But we also procrastinate for days, months, and years at a time. Conditions never seem quite right for the initiation of our project. We can't start to diet this week because we're going to have visitors who must be wined and dined. Next week, we're invited to a wedding feast. The week after, we're overwhelmed with work and feel the need to be easy on ourselves in other ways. We can't find any obstacles the week after that; but we decide to indulge for just a little longer. After all, it won't make any difference in the long run whether we begin to diet today or seven days from now. Seven days later, we're invited to another feast . . . Now, whether to diet is our own affair. We can choose to be as fat as we like. But *if* we've decided to lose weight, we are trapped in a monumental procrastination.

Formally, procrastination is a minor variation on the theme of resistance. In both traps, we hold back from an undertaking whose time has come. The difference lies in our intention toward the new task. When we resist, we don't recognize or accede to the legitimate demands of a new call to action. The emergency, opportunity, or interruption is imposed on us from the outside, and we refuse to place it on our agenda. But when we procrastinate, the call to action is our own.

We *want* to write the letter. We've already decided that we *will* write it. And still we hold back.

Another difference between resistance and procrastination is that the former finds us already occupied with a previous activity that we're reluctant to abandon in midstream. When we procrastinate, however, we don't appear to be busy with anything else. On the contrary, we may go out of our way to search out obscure and unimportant chores that give us an excuse for not getting started. This quest for make-work is very curious. Since it's we ourselves who have decided what to do next, what keeps us from beginning?

If we were waiting for conditions to become more favorable, our behavior would be considered fixated. Indeed, procrastinative activities bear a remarkable similarity to fixation. In both cases, we perform useless and disconnected acts such as twiddling our thumbs. In fixation, we twiddle to kill time until the moment for action arrives. But in procrastination, the moment for action has already come and still we twiddle. Then what are we waiting for?

The commonest cause for procrastination is undoubtedly a simple aversion to the new line of work. We know that it must be done, but we're loath to enter upon our allotted suffering. Standing at the end of the high diving board, our escape route blocked by a dozen taunting children, we know that we have to jump—that we *will* jump. But still we hesitate. Now holding back in the face of an unwelcome experience is eminently sensible if we don't ourselves accept its necessity. The condemned man who dawdles on his way to the gas chamber is not guilty of procrastination. In fact, to plunge into what we dislike before circumstances force our hand is the trap of anticipation. But once the necessity of suffering for a greater good has been acknowledged, holding back is a waste of time.

Aversion to the task can't be the whole story, however. Often enough, we procrastinate even when we know from experience that the new business won't be so awful once we get started. Once the letter is begun, it's relatively painless to continue to the end. There's a peculiar difficulty at the *beginning* that defies explanation in purely hedonistic terms. If the reluctance to start were wholly due to our aversion to the task, we would continue to experience it after we had begun. The second sentence of the letter would be just as stressful as the first. We would always be falling away from our engagement with the task and having again to overcome our procrastinative tendencies. But in fact the initial struggle with procrastination is usually enough to see us through. Of course, this is sometimes due to our discovery that the work wasn't as bad as we had expected. But often we know exactly what to expect before we begin. We've written letters many times before, and it's always been the same. We know that the job will prove to be easy once we get started. And still we delay. We may even procrastinate before enjoying our pleasures. We perform quaint but apparently useless cleansing and ordering rituals before settling down with a good book. Evidently, there are forces other than displeasure at work here.

One of these forces is a cumulative and unconscious *resistance* against abandoning the sum total of all the unfinished business in our life. When we procrastinate, we seem to be free of any prior agenda. But the experience of an unobligated moment is a rare event for those who haven't rid themselves of mental traps. Every project that has ever been on our agenda and not been brought to completion is on our agenda still. The press of more immediate concerns may have forced us to set these activities aside. But mental inertia doesn't simply evaporate when it's overcome. When the time arrives to start something new, the unfinished business of our life returns in a flood, clamoring for completion. Before we can turn our attention to reading a book, we need to *exorcize* ourselves. We have to tear ourselves away from the ever-present backlog of competing claims for our time.

We've seen that some mental traps involve us in projects that are literally endless. Striving to anticipate the future course of our life, we always have another day or another year to account for. The desire for absolute certainty or absolute precision requires us to amplify without end. The more we fall prey to traps like these, the greater will be our tendency to procrastinate before beginning something new. Once such a trap finds its way into our agenda, we have something to occupy us forever after. Every time we sit down to read or write a letter, we have to convince ourselves anew that our career plans won't suffer from being put aside for the evening. In the meantime, the world will continue to present us with new tasks; and we will get busier and busier, until we can no longer notice the taste of our food without engaging in a colossal struggle to clear our head.

It's this continuous burden of unfulfilled agendas that explains the most striking fact of all about our mental life: the fact that we're always thinking. Our mental engine is always in drive. As soon as we find ourselves between tasks, we're overwhelmed by ideas related to our inexhaustible fund of unfinished projects. We resume our anticipation of futures without end and our reversion to immutable past failures. We should have done this; we will do that. It isn't surprising that we procrastinate when a call to the new always finds us already occupied.

The burden of unfulfilled agendas also explains a rather odd behavioral phenomenon. We're in the habit of postponing the start of a new activity until some definite point in the future that is thought to be more opportune than the present. The oddity is that these points are selected for some *calendrical* property rather than for any characteristics that relate them to the activity itself. We decide to start our diet next Monday, as though a Monday were more suitable than a Thursday. We say that it "might as well" wait until the start of the week, whatever that means. New Year's resolutions belong to the same category of phenomena. If we're convinced that a course of action is desirable for us, why do we delay its adoption until the first of the year?

In part, such postponements are a device for permitting us to procrastinate while holding on to the illusion that we're dealing with the situation. Instead of *conducting* our business today, we *schedule* it for Monday and feel that it's already as good as done. After all, it will have been done by Tuesday. We need only endure the passage of time and it'll all be over. When Monday comes, of course, we can simply reschedule the task for a later date. In this way, we manage to procrastinate forever, remaining all the while convinced that we've let nothing slip.

But this doesn't yet explain our predilection for special calendar dates. Why do we more often reschedule the start of a new venture for a Monday rather than a Thursday? The reason is that many of the other activities on our agenda are tied to the official divisions of the calendar. The modern industrial week, for example, is rigidly divided into five days of work followed by two days of play. Work-related projects that would suffer from a two-day hiatus are therefore timed to end by Friday. As a result, we're less pre-occupied with ongoing business affairs on the following Monday than earlier in the week, and new projects find us less resistant. The long holiday season preceding New Year's Day is even more effective than the weekend in this regard. Many of our projects are geared to terminate before the holidays begin, and the accumulation of new obligations doesn't reach serious proportions until the first working day of the new year. In the interim, we feel less busy. Hence we're more inclined to embark on new ventures.

Is making New Year's resolutions a trap? It can be, if it's used merely as an excuse for postponing a necessary activity. But the backlog of unfinished business *is* lighter on New Year's Day, as a result of which new ventures *do* have a better chance of getting off the ground. Thus starting on New Year's Day may also be a strategic response to the backlog, in which case it *isn't* a trap. It's carrying around the backlog of past reversions and unfulfilled anticipations that's a trap. If we were entirely free of traps, we wouldn't carry around a burdensome backlog of unfinished business. There would then be no point to making New

Year's resolutions—starting on January 1 would be indistinguishable from starting on May 12. When we're totally free of traps, we live each day as though it were the start of a new millennium. But given that we *are* trapped by a backlog of unfinished business, it makes sense to schedule the start of new activities at a time when the backlog loses a little weight.

We've seen that the backlog of unfinished business provides an explanation for the basic phenomenon of procrastination: the reluctance to engage in a new project even though we seem to be unoccupied. The backlog also explains why we make New Year's resolutions and why we are always thinking. But it doesn't explain the most striking phenomenon of all relating to procrastination: the special difficulty at the *start* of new enterprises. The backlog functions as a source of tendencies that compete with the tendency to engage in the new project—but there's no reason to suppose that the competition is any stronger at the start of the new project than after the new project has already been begun. So why is writing the first sentence of a letter more difficult than writing the second sentence?

Here is a plausible explanation. Once the new

project has been begun, it generates its own inertia in amounts that are normally sufficient to overcome the inertial pull of the backlog. We've been assuming that a goal generates inertia as soon as we form the intention of achieving it. If this is so, then the inertia of the new project would have its countervailing effect right from the start. But suppose that starting a new project is a two-step procedure; first we formulate our intention to undertake the project, and second we perform the mental equivalent of pressing an "enter" key. Suppose also that the inertial tendency to complete what was begun is produced only when the intention is "entered." In effect, pressing the enter key is the first bit of work that needs to be done on any project. After the intention is entered, the new project will have its own inertia to keep it from being sidetracked by the backlog. But the first step of entering the intention has no such support. If this is how intentional action works, then we would expect to experience difficulties in getting started that disappear once we're on the way.

Procrastination is a resistance to engaging in a new task even though we *seem* to be unoccupied.

We've discussed one cause of this phenomenon: the inertial competition generated by the backlog of unfinished business. Here we seem to be unoccupied because what we're occupied with—the backlog—is always present. Another cause of procrastination is that the new task may find us already busy *doing-nothing*. Now doing-nothing, like the fixated activity of suspension, is indistinguishable from being unoccupied when viewed from the outside. Let's refer to the state of being unoccupied as the state of *not-doing-anything*. Not-doing-anything means not having an agenda, not trying to achieve any result. Doing-nothing, on the other hand, occurs when we *resolve* not to do anything. Like every other project, doing-nothing generates a certain amount of resistance against starting anything else. Viewed from the outside, it may appear that we hesitate to start even though we have nothing to do. In reality, the new task intrudes upon our planned nothingness. If we were really not-doing-anything, there would be nothing to intrude upon and we would not procrastinate.

Since doing-nothing causes us to procrastinate, it would be wise to give up the habit altogether. This doesn't mean that we should always be busy.

On the contrary, a certain amount of not-doing-anything is necessary in the economy of every living being. Even automobiles need to be turned off and allowed to cool. But doing-nothing is actually incompatible with not-doing-anything. It's a form of keeping busy. Not-doing-anything is a subtle frame of mind, however. As soon as we *resolve* to attain it, it's lost. Instead we make ourselves busy doing-nothing. We become guarded, tense, determined, and jealous of our time. Not-doing-anything isn't something we can *decide* to do. There are no instructions for it, since instructions can only tell us how to *do* things. The attempt not to do anything therefore always fails in its objective. This is the downfall of many vacations. The problem of how not to do anything will be discussed again in the last chapter.

We're especially liable to procrastinate when the task that lies ahead is very large. It's harder to start writing a novel than a letter, or to start washing a week's accumulation of dishes rather than a single teacup. The explanation of this phenomenon isn't as obvious as it first seems. To be sure, a big job is more arduous than a little one. But it doesn't automatically follow that *starting* the big job is more difficult than *starting* the little one. Objectively, it's just as easy to start washing a great heap of dishes as a single cup. In either case, we simply pick up an object and start to wipe. Finishing is another matter. But why are we more likely to wash the solitary cup without procrastinating than to wash the first item of a heap and then quit?

The culprit is a particular form of anticipation. Instead of deciding whether to *begin* the new job, we decide right from the start whether we will commit ourselves to the entire project. Since large enterprises call for a large investment of time and energy, it's natural that we entertain doubts before making such a commitment. But unless we're asked to sign a contract, there's no need for a commitment in the first place. The only question that needs an immediate reply is whether to start. Unless we *have to* make a commitment for some definite purpose, it's anticipatory to decide *now* that we *will* surely proceed to the end. After all, circumstances may change in such a way that finishing becomes unnecessary or undesirable, in which case our deciding will have been in vain. Even if the desirability of finishing is beyond all doubt, no purpose is served by obliging ourselves to finish. The value that persuades us to take the first step will presumably still be around to persuade us of the second step without the artificial aid of a commitment.

The real choice before us is whether to begin. And the beginning of even the vastest undertaking is as simple as fetching paper and pen or picking up a cup. Washing one cup is nothing to think twice about. And having washed it, we find the second cup just as inconsiderable. In this way, we eventually finish the job without subjecting ourselves to the useless and unpleasant burden of a self-imposed obligation. Of course we may throw in the sponge at any moment. But why deny ourselves this freedom? We can choose to go on if we wish. And if we quit, at least one cup will already be clean.

A proverb on our side for a change: the journey of a thousand miles begins with a single step.

If a company of angels came down to escort us to Heaven, we would undoubtedly procrastinate. For how can we make a clean break with the past when there are so many loose ends to tie up? We're only one semester away from our degree. The business is just beginning to make money.

We've almost finished reading *War and Peace*. Of course we want to go to Heaven. But it would be so much more convenient to postpone our trip until everything is settled. Then we can enter into our new estate with a clear mind.

But everything is *already* settled and always has been. The task before us is never more than one moment long. A moment later, we may be required to continue with what we're doing now. But that isn't our present concern. To be sure, we have ideas about what we will have to do in the future. But until the moment comes, these plans are no more than working hypotheses. Tomorrow everything may be entirely different.

We don't accumulate obligations. They come one at a time, and the previous one is canceled as soon as the next one takes effect. Our business is always already settled, our slate is always clean. There's no need to keep the angels waiting.

9.

We fall into the trap of *division* when we try to attend to two things at once. We participate in a conversation with one ear while at the same time trying to solve a financial problem that's been preying on our mind. Just as our financial musings draw close to a conclusion, the conversation turns to us—and the delicate structure of our thought is scattered to oblivion. When we return to the problem, we have to reconstruct the previously established results. At the same time, our contribution to the conversation is very boring.

The idea of doing two things at once needs some clarification. In a sense, we're always doing many things at the same time without suffering any ill effects. We continue to breathe while we're eating; we don't have to stop walking to look at the scenery. In these cases, however, at least one of the two activities doesn't require conscious attention. When we walk, we don't have to be continuously deciding to lift one leg and then the other. The proper sequence of events runs its course automatically. So long as they're automatic, we can perform any number of simultaneous acts. There seems to be no limit to our ability to turn skilled performances into automatized routines. An experienced automobile driver can get herself home in one piece, evidently stopping at every red light, while all the time absorbed in the contemplation of her business affairs. The sight of her own house suddenly looming before her sometimes takes her completely by surprise. And a trained pianist can play a creditable tune while chatting with friends.

But it's a basic law of the mind that we can't *consciously attend to* two things at once. Strictly speaking, attention is indivisible. When we try to be conscious of two things, it may appear that we're allotting a portion of our attention to each. But closer introspection reveals either (1) that the whole of consciousness is being made to shift back and forth between the two activities, or (2) that one of the activities is relegated to the unconscious, automatic mode of operation. Let's look at each of these two possibilities in turn.

If the sequence of thoughts relating to activity A is represented by A_1, A_2, A_3, and A_4, and the thoughts relating to activity B are B_1, B_2, B_3, and B4, the attempt to think them both at the same time results in a *mixed stream* of ideas that looks like this:

A1, A2, B1, A3, B2, B3, A4, B4

These oscillations from one topic to the other may, however, be so rapid that we have the illusion of simultaneity. One moment we're listening to the conversation, the next moment we revert to a private problem, and the moment after that we're listening again. Most of the oscillations pass unnoticed, and in retrospect it seems to us that we've been listening and thinking at the same time.

Now the commonest motive for *trying* to do two things at once is a desire to expedite our work. By dividing attention, we hope to complete two tasks in the time it would ordinarily take to complete just one. But since we have to think our conscious thoughts one at a time, this procedure can never save us any steps. There are four As and four Bs to work our way through, regardless of the order they're taken in. On the other hand, when we oscillate away from thought stream A, we can't expect to pick it up again exactly where we left off. We have to *pick up the threads* of the abandoned project. The interpolated activity B having distracted us, we must at least remind ourselves of the last conclusions before we are able to proceed. Often we need to repeat entire sequences of thought whose conclusion had already been arrived at. When attention is divided, we are returned again and again to the same starting point, from which place we must again and again rethink the same ideas. A more accurate portrayal of divided thought would be:

A1, A2, B1, A2, A3, B1, B2, B3, A2, A3, A4, B3, B4

Clearly it would be less arduous to do it like this:

A1, A2, A3, A4, B1, B2, B3, B4

Or like this:

B1, B2, B3, B4, A1, A2, A3, A4

This is why division is a trap.

Alternatively, the attempt to do two things at once may cause us to proceed with one of them at the unconscious level. We invest our private problem with continuous attention and fall into a pattern of automatic responding to someone we are conversing with: we smile and nod our head at everything he tells us. So long as the second task is thoroughly familiar and predictable, we will come to no harm. Some conversational partners never require more of us than an occasional token of approval. But if the course of events takes an unexpected turn, we may find ourselves in serious difficulties. We drive home with our mental gear in automatic, and the car in front of us screeches to a sudden halt. The bland spouter of conventionalities accuses us of wishing him dead, and we smile and nod our head.

Nevertheless, we must automatize some of our activities or else we could never do more than breathe. Unconsciousness per se is not an error. The trap is to try to do two things at once when we know that both of them require conscious attention. For then we can avoid the inefficiency of a mixed stream of thought only by the even less satisfactory route of letting our work on one of the tasks fall below the level of consciousness.

The fall from consciousness due to division is especially unfortunate when one of our activities is taken up for the sake of pleasure. In this case, we aren't so concerned with getting to the end as efficiently as possible. We don't mind having to take longer than necessary to eat a delicious dinner. But pleasure can't be relished without consciousness. If we try to think about our work while we're eating, we won't notice the taste of our food. Even if we manage to sustain a mixed stream, alternately paying attention to work and to pleasure, our pleasure will be reduced. And we won't do our best work.

Division is usually a secondary complication arising out of a previous case of anticipation or resistance, as pneumonia may develop from a cold. We enter into the divided state by taking on a second project before finishing or setting aside something already begun. We're busy with our algebra homework, but our thoughts begin to drift toward the romantic encounter we have planned for later in the evening. Now either the homework is more important to us right now, or romance is more important. We may decide this issue any way we wish. If getting the homework done now takes precedence over expediting our love life, we're guilty of anticipation. And if romance is an immediate imperative, we're guilty of resistance for not flinging aside our books and flying to our lover.

Now and then we may be unable to decide which of two activities is the more pressing. In that case, we should select one of them arbitrarily. For either order is preferable to a mixed stream of both at the same time. Forget about finances and enjoy the conversation. Or kick out the guests and return to the accounts. It doesn't matter which option you choose. Just don't get stuck in the middle.

In a previous chapter we saw that mental traps cause the amount of unfinished business in our life to be always on the increase. The world is always presenting us with new problems, but we're never quite finished with the old. We persist at tasks that have lost their meaning, amplify molehills into literally infinite mountains, revert to issues that are over and done with, and so on. As a result, there's always something to take our attention away from the task at hand. Every time we sit down to read a book, we're attacked by hordes of extraneous ideas relating to other times and other places. There are bills to be paid, children's teeth to be straightened, raises to be asked for, letters to write, ancient injuries to avenge, retirement plans to finalize . . . How can we simply sit and read when there's so much else happening at the same time?

We may live for years—even for a lifetime—in such a state of *chronic division*, always trying to hold all our unresolved problems in consciousness simultaneously instead of setting the burden down and picking up one item at a time. The penalty for chronic division is severe. Our skills and aptitudes are curtailed as surely as if we suffered brain damage—and we cease to experience pleasure.

A folk remedy for the ills of division is the habit of *saving the best for last*. As children, we ate the less favored sandwich crusts first, so that we might savor the soft middle portion without interruption. Now we open our mail in reverse order of interest—first the bills and advertising circulars, then the business letters, finally the personal correspondence. We put all our free hours at the end of the day, after all the chores are done, instead of taking a long break in the middle. Perhaps we design our whole life along this plan, deferring travels and adventures, the profound study of the saxophone, the cultivation of a garden—whatever truly attracts us—until after we've made ourselves financially secure.

The motive for this policy is very clear. If we live the best parts of life before the worst, our pleasure in them will be diminished by worries about what comes next. Better to get the sandwich crusts out of the way and not have them hanging over our head like a cloud! This is perfectly sound advice as far as it goes. If our pleasure in the best *will* be diminished by intrusions from the worst-to-come, it's better to get the worst over with first. But to permit such intrusions is already to fall into the trap of division. The situation is reminiscent of New Year's resolutions, discussed earlier. These are not themselves traps, but their usefulness is contingent on our having fallen into traps. Similarly, saving the best for last is not itself a trap. So long as we divide, we must defer our pleasures in order to enjoy them fully. But it's better not to divide in the first place. When we cease to divide, we no longer have a reason to save the best for last. We can take our pleasures any time we like.

Note that the technique of saving the best for last is ineffective in cases of chronic division. The chronic divider always has something preying on his mind that has to be settled before he can enjoy himself. The house is never *perfectly* clean, the future never *totally* secure. The attempt to get *everything* settled before enjoying the best of life results in *the perpetual postponement of pleasure*. And that surely is a trap. It's unwise to save the middle portion of the sandwich for the end when the crusts are infinitely long.

Another attempt to recapture the pleasure lost by division is to cancel all competing activities. We decide that we definitely will *not* make a difficult telephone call this evening, so that our enjoyment of dinner will be undiminished by intrusive thoughts. In this way we hope to lay the ghost to rest.

But this exorcism lands us immediately in the trap of *negative anticipation*: deciding prematurely *not* to do something. By a commitment not to make the telephone call, we purchase peace of mind at the cost of leaving an important chore undone. Peace of mind, however, may be had for free if only we cease to divide. We would enjoy our dinner at least as much if we simply put the issue of the telephone call entirely out of mind. There's no need to make a decision yet. If we approach the evening openly, with neither positive nor negative agendas, a moment may come when making the telephone call doesn't seem so odious. And then it will get done without our having had to think about it beforehand. Of course there can be no guarantees—the phone call may not get made. But nothing is to be gained by excluding the possibility of an easy solution right from the start.

Saving the best for last and negative anticipation are no more than symptomatic treatments for the division disease. Ultimately the only remedy that will restore our efficiency and our capacity for pleasure is to stop dividing. The technique for achieving this cure is *constant practice in doing one thing at a time*. Every single affair of the day is a suitable occasion for this important exercise. When we eat, we can practice just eating. When we wash the dishes, we can practice just washing. When we balance the checkbook, we can practice just doing arithmetic. Even the most insignificant acts—walking to the store, buying a newspaper—or the most odious—cleaning the toilet—have at least this element of value, if only we choose to harvest it: they're opportunities to practice single-mindedness.

The greater the penalty for division, the easier we find it to keep our attention on a single task. Most of us would have no difficulty keeping our undivided attention on driving down a narrow, winding mountain road on a stormy night. If life doesn't throw enough of these challenging circumstances our way, we would benefit by creating them intentionally. There's no more excellent tonic for division than to position ourselves halfway up a perpendicular cliff.

Once we've mastered the elementary exercises of remaining undivided during mountain climbing, tightrope walking, and hand-to-hand combat, we may graduate to the more demanding practices that arise in everyday life, such as eating and washing dishes. A still more advanced practice is to select an activity that is at once dull, useless, and thoroughly familiar, and to attend to it fully for a set period of time. Many of the practices that fall under the loose heading of meditation have exactly this purpose in mind. In some traditional approaches to mental development, students spend twenty minutes a day counting their breaths from one to ten over and over again. Mastery comes when they're not distracted from the count during the entire sitting. The benefit of this activity for everyday life may not be evident to those who don't attempt it. But neither are the benefits of lifting heavy weights and setting them down. Both are special exercises for strengthening our capacity to meet the requirements of living.

Counting breaths doesn't sound like a very difficult assignment. But it would be astonishing to find anyone who could count her breaths for twenty minutes without previous practice. The beginner would do well to start with five minutes and gradually build up. Even at five minutes she can't expect immediate success. Long before the time is up, she will have wandered off into the fathomless realm of her life's unfinished business.

When we catch our mind wandering away from the count, we should simply start again with the number one, as though nothing had happened. Every time we do this, we increase our ability to remain undivided as surely as each lift of the barbell improves our physique. After two or three months of daily practice, the increment in our mental efficiency and in the pleasure derived from daily life is so noticeable as to take almost all practitioners by surprise. It's hard to believe that such an intrinsically trivial activity can do so much. The same can be said of pumping iron.

The major obstacle to regular practice of this exercise is the impression that it's too boring to get through. This is nothing more than a rationalization. How can typists tolerate typing and assembly-line workers stick rods into sockets for eight hours if we can't endure five minutes of tedium? Can anything in the world possibly be so dull? It isn't boredom that makes us quit. We start to count our breaths and are shocked to discover that we can't perform what seems to be a trivially easy task. It's hard for us to admit that our mind is so totally out of control. So we tell ourselves that we *could* have done it if we wished, but that it was too boring. Then we go to our desk and make out bills for the next hour. This absurd rationalization may be dispensed with if we understand from the start that counting breaths doesn't come easily to anyone. We're bound to fail in our first attempts. If it were easy, there would be no point to it.

The Universe never asks more than one thing of us at a time. In the midst of a thousand desperate emergencies, we have only to attend to the *most* desperate emergency. The remaining 999 are simply not our concern. To be sure, disaster may strike if we don't get to them in time. But in this respect, the objective situation is really the same as in our unharried moments. Having taken care of all the business that seemed urgent, we may step out of the house and be run over by a truck. It's only because we don't think of it that the menace of trucks doesn't make us feel more busy. Trucks don't *present* themselves to us as a problem. But neither are we presented with the *known* problems that can't yet be dealt with. For the time being, they can also be put out of mind. We accomplish nothing useful by trying to hold them in consciousness. And the attempt to hold them interferes with our work on the task at hand.

In reality, there's never more than one thing to do. Being too busy is always a trap.

Acceleration

10.

Acceleration is the trap of acting at a faster than optimal rate. We repair a broken appliance so hurriedly that we make mistakes and the appliance immediately breaks down again. As a result, the resources that were devoted to this project have gone to waste. We might as well have done nothing at all.

Acceleration is a mirror image of procrastination. When we procrastinate, we are slow to start: we put off getting to work on the broken appliance with one excuse after another. When we accelerate, we're too quick to finish: we don't give the task its due measure of time and attention. These two traps are by no means incompatible. Sometimes we procrastinate at the beginning and then accelerate to the end.

We need to make a distinction here between acceleration and simply moving quickly, which will be called *hurrying*. We hurry but we do not accelerate when we run out of a burning building as fast as we can. On the other hand, an ordinary walking pace may already be accelerative when we're making our way through a minefield.

There are both advantages and disadvantages to doing things rapidly. The advantages are that (1) we get unpleasant business over with more quickly, (2) we sooner attain the goal we are working toward, and (3) we can sooner begin the next item of business in our life. For example, when we wash the dinner dishes as rapidly as we can, we may be motivated by the desire (1) to get a distasteful chore over with, (2) to have the dishes clean in time for a mother-in-law's imminent inspection, or (3) to give ourselves more time for a later and more important project.

The *dis*advantages of doing things too quickly are that (1) we are more likely to make errors along the way and (2) the activity is made more unpleasant by the irritant of having to rush. Washing the dishes as rapidly as we can, (1) we leave coffee stains on the bottoms of the cups and food particles between the fork tines, and (2) we increase the distastefulness of the chore by not taking the time to savor the positive elements of the experience. If the second disadvantage does not seem a great loss in the case of washing dishes, we may contemplate the cost of wolfing down what might have been a superb meal.

The advantages and disadvantages of hurrying have different weights in different circumstances. The disadvantage of increasing the chance of making an error by hurrying through a minefield outweighs the advantage of getting away from the field a few minutes sooner. But the disadvantage of leaving the dishes less than perfectly clean may be less important to us than the advantage of getting away from them sooner. There is no universal formula that tells us how fast we should work in every situation. Nevertheless, there's a class of circumstances in which hurrying is demonstrably non-optimal regardless of the values we assign to the various advantages and disadvantages. *If going faster increases one of the disadvantages without increasing any of the advantages, then we know that it's too fast.* At this point, hurrying has turned into acceleration.

Let's consider activities that are not unpleasant in and of themselves. In that case getting them over with quickly is not automatically an advantage, as it would be if the task were to carry a scorching hot plate to the table. But we might still wish to hurry (1) because the end result of our work is needed quickly or (2) because we have future business that can't wait for long.

There are no other reasons, however. If both the result of our work and the next order of business can wait, it's a trap to increase the risk of error and diminish the pleasantness of the work by going even the slightest bit too fast. With nothing pressing, we should take all the time that's needed to ensure a maximal performance.

Yet we're often tempted to rush by the sheer magnitude of things to come, even though we derive no benefit from doing so. We wolf down dinner to get to sex. Assuming that the opportunity for sex will not get up and go away, this behavior results only in a diminution of our total pleasure. If a leisurely dinner is worth 5 points on our pleasure scale, then a hurried dinner will earn us less than 5 points. Suppose its value to be 2, and suppose that sex is a 10. Then a leisurely dinner followed by sex is worth 5+10=15, while sex following a hurried dinner gives us only 2+10=12. To be sure, we get the 12 points sooner than the 15. But this is significant only if we have a reason to hurry—for example, if there's someplace else we have to get to immediately after sex.

Rushing through the activity at hand even though we're not pressed for time is *acceleration of the first kind*.

If the present activity can wait, it's a trap to rush through it even if the next order of business *can't* wait. For here we could simply postpone the present project until a more leisurely time. Instead of hurriedly trying to finish a newspaper article before the commercial is over and the TV show begins, we can read it at our leisure when the show is done. In these *accelerations of the second kind,* there's no need to rush through what we're doing because we needn't be doing it now in the first place.

What possesses us to rush when we are not pressed for time? Significantly, acceleration is always preceded by a *divided* state of mind. We wouldn't rush through an innocuous or pleasant task unless we had some other project or condition in mind at the same time. We wolf down our dinner because we're thinking of the after-dinner sex while we eat, and we rush through the newspaper article because we have an eye on the TV show to come—only one minute left! thirty seconds! twenty! If we had no agenda for the future, we would have no place to rush to. We would abide in the present task and make the best of it.

The unpleasantness of division causes us to resort to various folk remedies whose secondary

complications are often as injurious as the original disease. With two things on our mind, we may
save the best for last, so that we're no longer bur-
dened by other concerns when we get to it.
Alternatively, we may try to unburden ourselves
immediately by an act of *negative anticipation*,
canceling one of the two activities so that we have
only one thing to think about. Or we may *accelerate* through the first activity in order to arrive
more quickly at the undivided state. Acceleration
is a misguided strategy for coping with division.

We observe the link between acceleration and
division when a child arrives at a playground
after a long and bitter absence. Attracted simultaneously to all the rides, he can't fully enjoy any
one of them without divisive longings for the others. So he takes one quick run down the slide,
rushes to the monkey bars where he clambers to
the top and immediately descends, goes up and
down on the seesaw three times, and runs off to
the swings. Having fulfilled his agenda as rapidly
as possible, he returns to a single piece of equipment and gives it his undivided attention.

The divided state that leads to acceleration is
in turn caused by either anticipation or resistance.
Anticipation ultimately produces accelerations

of the first kind, and resistance is responsible for accelerations of the second kind. It's instructive to see how these two sequences of mental traps develop.

If we had only the present task in mind, we wouldn't rush because there would be no other condition to rush toward. Thus the first step on the road to acceleration is a thought about some future activity. Eating dinner, we begin to contemplate the even greater pleasures of the bedroom that await us. If the future project can wait, thinking about it now when we already have something to do is *anticipatory*. Furthermore, the anticipated project competes for our attention with the task at hand, creating a state of division. And then we rush through the present activity to terminate our division. The possibility of enjoying dinner having been undermined by anticipation, we try to get it over with as quickly as possible. Yet we have all the time in the world. This is acceleration of the first kind.

On the other hand, if the present task can wait but a future project cannot, we're guilty of *resistance* for not dropping the former altogether. The commercial is just about over, and still we hold on to the idea of finishing our article.

Clutching the old as the new forces itself upon us, we're again precipitated into a state of division, and again we try to shorten our pain by rushing through the task at hand. In this case, however, the better course would be simply to postpone the task at hand. This is how acceleration of the second kind comes about.

In sum, we have the following relationships:

anticipation ⇨ acceleration of the first kind

division ⇨

resistance ⇨ acceleration of the second kind

The steps on the journey of life appear one at a time and at their own pace. If we lunge ahead or lag behind, we stumble and fall. Lunging ahead is anticipation and acceleration of the first kind. Lagging behind is resistance and acceleration of the second kind.

Festina lente—make haste slowly—another proverb on our side.

—

We've seen that both anticipation and resistance often develop into chronic conditions. We may always be trying to anticipate another step into the future, and our backlog of unfinished business may always be a source of resistance to the new. Either of these maladies may be further compounded by *chronic acceleration*, a condition in which we're perpetually rushing through whatever we are doing in order to get to the next thing.

Chronic acceleration is the state of always being on the way to somewhere else. We rush through the main course to get to the dessert. We rush through dessert because we can't live with the dirty dishes. We rush through the dishes to get to our book. If the book is interesting, we're beckoned by each page to rush through its predecessor—an acceleration of the first kind. If the book is dull, we read as quickly as we can to get it over with—an acceleration of the second kind. Life is just one damn thing after another.

On a larger timescale, we see each period of our life as mere preparation for the next. We have to finish our education as quickly as possible so that we may embark on our professional career. We must achieve professional success as soon as we can so that we may begin to enjoy status and security. After success comes a mad dash to find something else to absorb our energies. And having invented a new problem for ourselves, we rush to find the solution as quickly as we possibly can. It seems that the present is always something to get over. We fail to see the logical consequence of living like this: if we're always getting the present over with, then the whole of life becomes something to get over, like a flu. Chronic acceleration is a headlong gallop toward death.

If our work is infinite—if it will never be at an end—then what's the point of rushing? Expediting the end of one chore earns us only the privilege of beginning the next. Infinity minus one is still infinity. Therefore speed can't improve our condition. We might as well take our time with everything we do.

Chronic acceleration can so accustom us to rushing that we no longer need an excuse for it. Even if the activity is pleasant and we have nothing else to do, we automatically try to get it over with as quickly as we can. We stroll urgently through the park, as though our aim were not to stroll but to *have* strolled. In this state of *empty acceleration*, we take it for granted that there must be *some* reason to rush, even though we can't immediately call it to mind. Empty acceleration is the experience of pure, unconceptualized urgency.

11.

We've seen that we often think about our problems too soon or too late, too much or too little. The most elusive error, however, is to concern ourselves with topics that needn't be thought about at all. In the twin traps of *regulation* and *formulation*, we adopt attitudes toward issues that don't touch our lives, make decisions about events that are just as well left to whim or chance, or purposelessly keep up a blow-by-blow description of the passing scene, as though the movie of reality stood in need of narration.

Whether a particular superfluity of thinking is regulative or formulative depends on the quality of our mental processes. We need to make a distinction here between *descriptive* and *prescriptive* thinking. Descriptive thought says what a thing is; prescriptive thought intends that something be. When we make a mental note that the door is open, we're thinking descriptively; when we resolve to shut it, we're thinking prescriptively. *Regulation* is the trap of making useless prescriptions; *formulation* is useless description. We'll examine regulation in this chapter and formulation in the next.

A purely descriptive idea leaves us at rest. When we note that the door is open, the matter is at an end. Prescriptive thought, however, urges us to adopt a line of action. Having told ourselves to shut the door, we feel the need to carry out our orders.

But prescriptions aren't the only wellsprings of action. Living beings are active even when they're not telling themselves what to do. A mosquito is unlikely to be wending its way through the world by means of prescriptions ("And now to suck his blood!"); yet it manages to sustain a fairly energetic lifestyle. And we humans too are always scratching, stretching, sniffing, and shifting about without telling ourselves to do so. The non-prescriptive sources of action, whatever they are, may simply be called *impulse*. Our activity, then, is either *impulsive* or *prescriptive*, depending on which of the following patterns it adheres to:

Impulsive:

impulse ⇨ action (⇨ descriptive thought)

Prescriptive:

(impulse ⇨) prescriptive thought ⇨ action

The parenthetical terms in each case refer to optional events. Scratching on impulse, we may also note descriptively that we are scratching; but our activity doesn't require such a notation. And a prescribed movement may also be preceded by a redundant impulse to do the same thing, as when we happen to be hungry on our lunch hour.

These modes of action correspond to what an antiquated philosophical tradition once called our "lower" and our "higher" natures, respectively. Our two natures were conceived to be in a state of perpetual conflict, and mental health was defined as the absolute and permanent victory of prescription over impulse. Although antiquated, this view is by no means extinct.

Not surprisingly, some things are best done by prescription and some by impulse. Each mode of action has its own province. For example, projects that require the coordinated efforts of several people usually have to be approached prescriptively. If you and I are to carry a large sofa down the stairs, we must establish and adhere to certain ground rules. I can't let go of my end simply because I have an impulse to rest. On the other hand, when we're on vacation and free of any scheduled obligations, it would be foolish to continue to eat lunch precisely at noon regardless of whether we're hungry. Here the rule of impulse makes our life more pleasant without bringing any disadvantages in its wake.

We fall into the trap of regulation when we prescribe our behavior in a situation where impulse would be a better guide. We regulate when we eat simply because it's lunchtime, go to bed because it's bedtime, or decide ahead of time how we will greet intimate friends who would no longer be surprised at anything we might blurt out. To be sure, we may also commit the opposite error of acting impulsively when we should be following a prescription. We don't want our surgeon or our airline pilot to be guided by the whim of the moment. We want these people to have a *plan*. But overimpulsiveness is not a mental trap. By definition, mental traps are injurious habits of thought. Overimpulsiveness, however, is an insufficiency of thought. Like bankruptcy or breaking a leg, it's a misfortune of another order.

Prescribing our behavior is a trap even when prescription is as good a guide as impulse. That is to say, impulse wins if it's a tie. There are two reasons for this. The first is that prescribing is a species of *work*—it's something that happens only if we *do* it. Impulse, however, arises by itself, without requiring any effort on our part. If both modes of functioning are equally effective, we might as well relax and let impulse do it. The same can be said of the far more frequent situation wherein we *can't tell* whether a prescriptive or an impulsive approach would be more desirable.

The second reason that impulse wins ties is particularly important. In the course of discussing the previous nine traps, I've had several occasions to refer to the phenomenon of *mental inertia*. This is the tendency of agents to continue with what was begun, just because it was begun. It's clear that the inertial tendency is a major cause of falling into mental traps. It propels us into persistence by causing us to keep working after the value of the goal is lost; it makes us fixate by causing us to keep working when there's nothing to be done; it lands us in resistance by causing us to keep working toward an old goal when it's time to do something new; and so on.

The inertia to complete project X is produced when we adopt the *intention* to do X—equivalently, when we *prescribe* X for ourselves. *Impulse*, on the other hand, is inertialess. If we adopt the project of whistling "Row, Row, Row Your Boat," we will experience at least a little bit of difficulty in stopping in midstream (as it were). But there's no difficulty in stopping if we start to whistle the same tune impulsively, without *telling* ourselves to do it. This is a reason to prefer impulsivity to prescription, all other things being equal. *By acting on impulse, we avoid the inertia that can so easily precipitate us into mental traps.*

Some ways of regulating our behavior are subtler than others. The most uncouth is simply to *ignore the impulse* and follow a prescription when impulse is the better guide. Our previous examples of regulation, such as eating lunch simply because it's noon, all belong to this category. Some of us are so entirely ruled by prescription that we seem no longer to be aware that impulses exist. We shave every day (or refrain from shaving), wear a belt (or suspenders), drink coffee (or tea), and watch the news (or the soap operas) without even asking ourselves whether these routines are in accord with our current impulses. We've decreed that we shall be shaven and belted, and no amount of discomfort, distaste, or inconvenience can change the law.

When we rediscover the realm of spontaneous, undictated impulse, we naturally begin to work at loosening the stranglehold of universal prescription. But early attempts to regain our spontaneity invariably miscarry in curious ways. Instead of simply permitting ourselves to be guided by impulse, we institute prescriptions of an ever subtler order. Having ceased to ignore the impulse, we pass through a phase of *regulating the impulse*— that is, of finding laws that describe our impulsive behavior, and then turning these descriptive laws into new prescriptions. After years of eating dinner in an arbitrarily prescribed fashion, we discover that we enjoy the salad more when it comes *after* the main course. So we change over to a new prescription that ostensibly takes our true impulses into account: "Salads after entrées!"

In this type of regulation, impulse is no longer totally ignored; but it still isn't permitted to govern actions belonging to its rightful sphere. Instead of directly following our inclinations, we consult a prescriptive rule that's supposedly "true" to these inclinations. But no function is served by making a rule out of what happens naturally. If it's true that we always enjoy salads more after the main course, impulse alone will cause us to eat them at the right time. Regulating the impulse is like vowing to continue to breathe. At the very least, it's a redundant procedure, a waste of effort.

At the worst, regulating the impulse may lead us as far astray as totally ignoring the impulse. For our inclinations aren't always so predictable as the desire to breathe. After preferring to eat our salad after the entrée for a number of years, we may find our tastes have changed. But if we're in the habit of consulting the regulations instead of letting impulse rule, we may not notice the change for a long time. Yet because the regulations were originally based on observed patterns of impulsivity, we continue to believe that we're acting "on impulse." In this condition we're even more befuddled than when the impulse was ignored right from the start, for then at least we entertained no such illusions.

Many of us are unable to discriminate between the regulation of impulse and impulsive action itself. We think that we're doing what comes naturally when in fact we are first noting what comes naturally and then putting it in the form of a rule for better living. We decide that we like company more than solitude, city life more than country life, bright colors more than subdued colors—and then we rigidly adhere to these regulations in the name of pleasing ourselves. If we really did please ourselves, our behavior would change as soon as our inclinations changed. But the regulations based on our inclinations inevitably lag behind. We're still surrounding ourselves with bright colors and crowds of people in the city long after these things only give us a headache. This is how the regulation of impulse leads to the trap of persistence.

After we've seen through the trap of regulating our impulses, we may yet fall into any of three increasingly devious modes of regulation—*reflecting the impulse*, *reading the impulse*, and *null regulation*. Each of these is a type of prescription that masquerades as impulse.

In *reflecting the impulse*, we give up trying to second-guess the twists and turns that will be taken by our impulsive life. We do not vow to eat our salad either after the main course or before. Instead, we vow that we will do it whenever we wish. We make it into a regulation that we will follow our impulses in this matter. We tell ourselves that we will eat when we are hungry, rest when we are tired, and so on. Now regulations of this type do keep our behavior more or less in line with our impulses. But they're still a waste of time. When impulse rules, there's no need for any conscious intervention whatsoever. Behavior follows impulse of its own accord. If only we remain inwardly silent, we *will* eat when we're hungry and rest when we're tired. By reflecting the impulse, we depart from the pattern for straightforwardly impulsive action:

(impulse to do X) $\Rightarrow$ (do X)

and substitute for it a baroque variety of prescriptive activity:

(impulse to do X) $\Rightarrow$ (prescription: "when the impulse to do X is felt, do X") $\Rightarrow$ (do X)

Instead of feeling hungry and then eating, we feel hungry, consult the prescription that we should eat when we are hungry, and *conclude* that we should eat. Clearly, this is an entirely useless procedure. Its only effect is to disrupt the spontaneous flow of impulsivity. We still eat when we're hungry, but our actions are "sicklied o'er with the pale cast of thought." Instead of acting like this:

our behavior looks and feels like this:

Our actions are only *approximations* of impulsivity.

The trap of *reading the impulse* is another step closer to true spontaneity. Here we no longer interpolate a redundant universal rule between impulse and action. But neither are we yet content to be guided directly by impulse. We deem it necessary at least to translate the impulse into a single prescriptive thought. Instead of:

(impulse to do X) ⇨ (do X)

we have:

(impulse to do X) ⇨ (prescription: "do X!")
⇨ (do X)

Instead of simply eating when we are hungry, we note our hunger and tell ourselves to eat.

Reading the impulse is an advance over reflecting the impulse, in that a certain amount of useless mental work has been thinned out. We no longer pretend to be following a general law. But we still insist on telling ourselves what to do when we would do the same thing spontaneously. We are like an inept corporate executive who, fearful of losing his grip, insists that all directives be funneled through his office, if only for a rubber stamping. Impulse speaks to us in the language of feelings, and we echo it inanely on the level of prescriptive thought: "Eat . . . drink . . . go to sleep . . . relax . . . have fun . . . have an orgasm . . . smile . . ."

The last refinement of regulation is the trap of *null regulation*. Having perceived the uselessness of even reading the impulse, we vow henceforth to let impulse rule in its proper domain without imposing any intermediate prescriptions whatever. And then when impulse makes itself felt, we invoke the prescription that permits it to rule. We feel hungry or tired, tell ourselves not to prescribe in such a situation, and then eat or rest. We tell ourselves to be spontaneous. We resolve to go with the flow. In effect, we prescribe that we shall not be prescriptive. Of course this directive can never be fulfilled, because it's self-contradictory. We can no more command spontaneity of ourselves than slaves can be set free by an act of their masters. Slaves must free themselves, and spontaneity can be allowed to emerge only by itself. Instead of achieving genuine impulsivity of this form:

(impulse to do X) ⇨ (do X)

we fall prey to yet another redundant prescription:

(impulse to do X) ⇨
(prescription: "let impulse rule! ") ⇨ (do X)

Null regulation is prescriptive action in its most exquisite disguise. At no point do we actually tell ourselves what to do, as in the previous varieties of regulation. We simply tell ourselves to follow our impulses. But if we must *tell* ourselves to follow them, the final authority for what we do is still prescriptive. We've likened the trap of *reading* the impulse to an executive's having to approve every decision made by his subordinates.

In null regulation, the executive only pretends to give his subordinates a greater measure of independence. He no longer explicitly approves or disapproves of their decisions. Instead, he looks at each decision in turn and indicates whether they shall have the freedom to decide in this particular case. The net result is the same as before. Granting freedom of choice on a case-by-case basis *after* the decision has been made is equivalent to approving or disapproving. It's only a trick.

At this stage in our struggle against regulation, we're apt to say things like "The only rule is that there are no rules." Like the skeptic who is certain that nothing can be known for sure, we're oblivious to the untenability of our position.

What causes us to resort to cumbersome prescriptions when effortless impulsivity would suffice? There can be only one motive. We have lost all confidence in impulsivity as a guide for action. Some of us are no longer aware that impulses are even *capable* of guiding action, whether for good or ill. We think that as soon as we cease to tell ourselves what to do, we will stop dead in our tracks, having no basis upon which to choose one action over another. We make our way through the world by perpetually kicking our own behinds, first to the left and then to the right.

And after we recognize both the existence and the legitimacy of certain classes of impulse, we still insist on passing each individual case to our prescriptive apparatus for final approval. We're afraid that raw impulse, unchecked by prescription, will make our actions chaotic, absurd, or downright dangerous. If we don't tell ourselves what to do at every moment, we may wander away from home, forget to urinate, or stick a thumb in our eye. This view is utterly refuted by the ordered existence of the non-prescribing "lower" animals, not to mention trees and plants. To be sure, rabbits and daffodils can't build rockets to the moon or hold committee meetings. But we're not always busy with rockets and committees ourselves.

12.

ormulation is the trap of indiscriminately saying or thinking something just because it seems to be true. We're not content to marvel at a spectacular sunset. We also have to *note* that it's a Marvelous Sunset, if only to ourselves. We say "Oooh" and "Aaah" and "Isn't it a Marvelous Sunset"? and "Aren't we Having a Good Time?" If a news reporter or a myopic friend had asked us to comment on the quality of the sunset, a brief description would be nothing more than benevolence. But what, exactly, is the point of describing these things to *ourselves*?

Concept-making and describing are powerful tools. Without them, we would derive very little benefit from the experience of others. One after another, we would nibble at the same deadly fungus and fall into the same ravine. We would have no help in discovering the orderliness of the seasons, the movements of the sun and the moon, and the stages of human life. In sum, we would be indistinguishable from any other large land mammal. Nevertheless, there are also disadvantages to

saying what a thing is. We fall into the trap of formulation when we bring these disadvantages
upon ourselves without compensation.

The most obvious disadvantage of formulation
is that it leads to *division*. Every time we describe
or evaluate an experience before it's over, we are
doing two things at once. On the one hand, we're
watching a sunset; on the other hand, we're talking
or thinking about it. We've already seen how division destroys pleasure. We can't really watch a
sunset and evaluate it at the same time, for the
activity of evaluating takes our attention away
from the sensual experience. The moment we say
"Isn't it Marvelous?" we're no longer marveling.

Our experience is even more drastically curtailed if we fall prey to *public formulation*, wherein
we strive to write it all down or tell it to a friend
before we forget. In this trap, we act as though
experiences counted for nothing until they
entered the public domain. A beautiful sunset or
an entertaining thought becomes a burden to be
unloaded as quickly as possible. We rush away
from pleasure immediately upon perceiving it, so
that we may communicate it to the world. Good
news oppresses us until we lay hold of pen and
paper or a receptive ear. We "can't wait" to tell.

Photography introduces a new dimension to the art of public formulation. There are people who curse their fate for coming upon an interesting sight when they've left their camera at home. They would rather have *nothing*. With the advent of home video equipment, we will soon be recording every moment of the day in three dimensions and stereophonic sound. And we'll spend the next day watching the playback, and the day after that watching ourselves watch the playback . . .

The public formulator supposes that experiences don't count unless they make an impression beyond the confines of his own mind. Those of us who are free of this delusion may yet labor under the equally groundless assumption that experiences don't count unless we formulate them *inwardly*. We remember Socrates' advice: the unexamined life is not worth living. We think that if we don't *note to ourselves* that we're having a valuable experience, we might as well not have it at all. This causes us to engage in *private formulation*.

But Socrates was the principal architect of a disastrous confusion between *thinking* and *consciousness* that has ever since bedeviled Western culture. As we demonstrated in the first chapter, thinking and consciousness are entirely different mental processes. We often think unconsciously, and we may be fully conscious without entertaining a single idea. Now it's true that we have to be *conscious* of our experience in order to enjoy it. We can't marvel at a sunset that passes unnoticed. But it isn't necessary to *think* about the experience, or to speak its name. On the contrary, the never-ending litany of formulas that usually accompany experiencing—"Good food! Yum-yum! This is terrific!"—serve only to diminish pleasure by dividing our attention.

Certain of life's experiences are not merely diminished by formulation. Their very existence depends on our refraining from speaking their name, even in the privacy of our own mind. They are regions of the Universe that remain forever closed to the formulator. For example, the enjoyment of humor requires us to suspend our formulative tendencies. We can't simultaneously *experience* funniness and describe what makes it funny. The explanation of a joke doesn't get laughs. If we insist on saying what everything is, we will always be grim.

A textbook-perfect example of an experience killed by the slightest brush with formulation is the aesthetic appreciation of mystery. Connoisseurs of this experience are rare nowadays. We move so quickly to fit every situation into our conceptual scheme that we no longer know the pleasures of bafflement and speechless wonder. We see mystery only as a problem to be alleviated by "further research." We await the day when science takes the mystery "out of" acupuncture, hypnosis, or flying saucers, supposing this to be an unalloyed good. But the tailoring of conceptual schemes to fit phenomena (or vice versa) is only one of the games in town. To be sure, it's a game that has enjoyed a great deal of prestige in the last few hundred years. The pursuit of intellectual knowledge has the lofty status that was once reserved for the service of God. But knowledge, like every other commodity, has its costs, and it's an unwise shopper who pays more than a thing is worth. We wouldn't willingly lose our eyesight for the knowledge of what our neighbors ate for breakfast this morning. And laundering the Universe clean of mystery is very much like going blind. For mystery isn't just an absence of knowledge—it's an experience in its own right, palpable as an itch.

The key to the arcane realm is a mind free of useless opinions.

—

Our needless *descriptions* of the world have an uncanny knack of turning into arbitrary *prescriptions*, catapulting us from *formulation* into *regulation*. We pointlessly tell ourselves that we're Cleaning the House, intending only to describe our present condition. But immediately we feel as though we're under an obligation to ensure the continuing veracity of our words. We ruefully turn down invitations to other activities on the grounds that we are, after all, Cleaning the House. We can't stop to chat with a friend because we're Going Somewhere. We won't take the smelly garbage out of the kitchen because we've already begun to Rest. From the fact that something *is*, we jump to the conclusion that it *must* be.

Sometimes we formulate enduring traits for ourselves such as Social Ineptitude, Excitability, or an abiding Aversion to Vegetables. These descriptions too are quickly transformed into their prescriptive counterparts. But in this case the obligations incurred are lifelong. Having committed ourselves to the view that we're "the sort of person who" hates vegetables, we're called upon again and again to sustain the truth of our self-description. We can't make ourselves constitutionally Averse to Vegetables or Socially Inept in one fell swoop. The feat requires a disciplined adherence to the formula-turned-regulation we have adopted. We must perpetually resist the stream of impulses from within and invitations from without to act in new ways. Self-definition is self-mutilation on a heroic scale.

This isn't to say that we lack all consistency of personality. Even if we cease to formulate our character, an external observer will be able to detect recurring patterns in our choices and reactions. But we can't formulate the results of such observations for *ourselves* without producing certain drastic effects. The opinion that one is excitable or socially inept is itself a major cause of excitability or social ineptitude. Beliefs about the self are self-fulfilling prophecies, and the fulfillment of the prophecy in turn welds us ever more strongly to the belief that engendered it. Our formulas for ourselves are at once true and profoundly misleading. The Man Who Never Eats Vegetables is quite correct—he never eats vegetables. But if he didn't hold this view of himself, he might actually indulge in an occasional carrot.

It's impossible for us to give an objective account of ourselves. The situation is reminiscent of the uncertainties of observation encountered in contemporary physics. We can never determine the exact location and speed of a subatomic particle because these quantities are altered by the very act of trying to observe them. And we can never describe ourselves as we really are because we are changed by the very act of description. We can only *be* who we are. This is very difficult for some people to accept.

Why do mere descriptions turn so quickly into prescriptions without good cause? Once again, our unhappy relationship with impulse is to blame. The impulse to leave the peas and carrots on our plate fully accounts for our not eating them. There's no problem here. But unless we're able to deduce our behavior from a rule, we feel that we're acting "unreasonably." We are intimidated by demands for rational explanations: *why* didn't we eat our vegetables? Our difficulty is that most of what we do in the course of a day can be neither justified nor condemned by an appeal to general principles. There's nothing in the Bible or in secular law that dictates an attitude toward vegetables. Then where will the pertinent prescription come from? Living a purely prescriptive life is like lifting oneself by one's bootstraps. The *description* of what we're doing provides a convenient handle or, more aptly, a life jacket to a drowning man. If we're the "sort of person" who doesn't eat vegetables, then we can explain everything!

Premise 1:   I'm the sort of person who doesn't eat vegetables.

Premise 2:   These peas and carrots are vegetables.

Conclusion: Therefore, I do not eat them.

Now our reason is satisfied: we haven't acted haphazardly. But there is a price. When an unexpected attraction to zucchini stirs faintly in our breast, we will deny it in the name of consistency and we'll miss a tasty dish.

We can avoid most mental traps simply by fixing our attention on the present task. While we're washing the dishes or walking to the store, there's no need to think about what will happen next or what has happened before. There's only this dirty spoon, this street scene before us. Every departure from the here and now is a trap. If our thoughts fly away to the future, we are fixating or anticipating. If we go back to the past, we revert or resist. But there's also an avenue of departure from the present—from *this*—that strays neither into the future nor into the past. It leads vertically from this to "This"—from washing the dishes to *telling* ourselves that we are Washing the Dishes. These thoughts are just as useless and disruptive as anticipations of twenty years hence or reversions to twenty-year-old grievances.

Formulation is the last mental trap to go. We may clearly see how life is possible without keeping the future or the past constantly in mind. But at least, we think, the *present* must be kept in mind. We can forgo knowing what comes next, but at least we have to know what's happening *now*. But assuming that circumstances don't change, once a decision has been made to do something, it serves no purpose to keep what we are doing in mind. When we're cleaning the house, it's enough to dust the table and make the bed. Perpetually reminding ourselves that we are Cleaning the House drains us of energy, divides our attention, and causes us to resist new alternatives.

When we're occupied with *this*, there's nothing that needs to be kept in mind. Even "This" is saying too much.

Keeping Out of
Mental Traps

13.

Now that we've developed some skill in detecting traps, how do we manage to get out of them? Let's look in on a moment when we *are* out of them. All but the most blighted lives are blessed now and then with brief intervals of freedom from mental traps. We may be walking to the mailbox as we have countless times before when we suddenly realize that we are *just* walking to the mailbox. For a moment, there's nothing else in the world but the spring of our step and the sun on our face. The present moment fills our consciousness entirely, banishing yesterday and tomorrow, hope and regret, plans, schemes, should-have-beens, what-ifs, and let-me-justs. We experience a delightful sense of lightness. The customary forced march through a field of molasses comes to a halt, and we glide. We haven't a care in the world. There's nothing to keep track of, nothing to remember, nowhere to get to, nothing to get over with. This moment exists all by itself. Why don't we simply continue to live like this for the rest of time?

The answer is obvious. We don't believe that life can be so simple. While we glide, who's minding the store? It seems to us that our countless outstanding problems and projects must suffer from this sort of neglect. The good things we wish to secure must immediately begin to recede from us unless we keep them in their place by perpetually renewing our commitment to them. And the dire circumstances we want to avert must come closer unless we keep them at bay by our eternal vigilance. Living entirely in the present seems to us like holding our breath—perhaps we can do it for a minute or two on a dare, but it can't be a way of life. After a few untrapped steps, we become frightened and plunge back into the sea of familiar troubles. There's work to be done.

Is life simple or complex? Do we need elaborate calculations and prescriptions to get through, or will things work out as well in the end if we let impulse rule and just run free? As with all issues of ultimate importance, there's something to be said for both sides. On the one hand, it isn't true that we must *always* be vigilant, *always* calculating. Our situation doesn't *automatically* deteriorate as soon as we turn our head. At least sometimes, we may allow ourselves the luxury of perfect spontaneity. We won't automatically wander off the edge of a cliff as soon as we cease to push our lives from behind along a predetermined track.

On the other hand, there are cliffs; and when we skirt close to one, we must begin to calculate our steps. There are times when we can afford to be spontaneous, free, and impulsive; and there are times we have to be vigilant, calculating, and prescriptive. The question is how to key into one mode of operation and out of the other. This *switching problem* is the most fundamental problem of human life.

From one perspective—let's call it the perspective of *modern consciousness*—this problem poses a formidable dilemma. At time X, while we're functioning in the prescriptive mode, we may judge that current conditions make it safe for us to switch to the impulsive mode. But of course, even though it's safe to be impulsive now, at X, there will come a time Y when we will need to revert to prescription. And if we permit the impulsive mode to take over, how will we recognize when moment Y arrives? Wandering aimless and free through the desert, we will not notice when we cross the point which takes us too far from home base, and we will die. The answer, says modern consciousness, is always to keep our distance from home base in mind, never to run totally free. Modern consciousness solves the problem of how to key in and out of prescription by *leaving the prescriptive mode running all the time—even when it isn't needed*. Prescription may not be needed now; but if the reins are handed over to impulse, the prescriptive mode may not be keyed back in when it *is* needed.

It's inevitable that such a strategy should lead to mental traps. To be trapped, by definition, is to perform mental work that isn't needed. And the strategy of modern consciousness is to be working all the time. We feel we must always stay "on top" of the situation, just in case. The various traps are no more than different ways of trying to stay on top.

There are other solutions to the problem of keying in and out of the prescriptive mode. For one, we may hand over the keying function to an external agency that, we trust, will be vigilant for us and turn our prescriptive apparatus on and off as necessary. Those who accept the absolute authority of another person (mother, guru), an organization (the church, the government), or a system of ideas (psychoanalysis, Marxism) have much less of a problem with mental traps. When the authority tells them to do mental work, they work. And when the authority declares a holiday, they can really and truly rest, secure in the knowledge that someone else is minding the store.

This is the great consolation of belonging to a religion, whether spiritual or secular: it permits us to lay down our burden. Biblical fundamentalists and doctrinaire Marxists are better able than we are to sustain and enjoy the giddy sense of life's simplicity and freedom from agendas. They can accept whatever the future will bring. They have no need to shape it according to their will, because they're certain that Marx or the Bible will prove to be an adequate guide in any eventuality. True believers don't need to study mental traps.

This is how most people lived in simpler ages. They learned the values and traditions of their society in one piece, and these values governed their actions forever after. It never occurred to them to *choose* a way of life, since there were no examples of alternatives around them. And because they had no choice, they felt entirely free. This archaic mode of being, still enjoyed by the contemporary true believer, is qualitatively different from the life of modern consciousness. Let's call it *traditional consciousness*.

Traditional consciousness disappears when external authority ceases to be monolithic. As soon as there are two bibles, we can no longer be perfect fundamentalists. For whether we wish it or not, we must choose, on the basis of our own lights, which bible we're going to follow. And contemporary society presents us with innumerable candidates for biblehood. This makes it exceedingly difficult to become a true believer nowadays. Even if we definitely opt for one bible or another and follow its dictates to perfection, the fact that we've chosen distinguishes us still from a bona fide true believer. For we must have chosen on the basis of some *criterion*—rationality, intuition, it doesn't matter which—and so, whether we desire it or not, it's this inner criterion that remains the foundation of our action. We can persuade ourselves to accept a bible as a perfectly correct and perfectly complete guide to living, but we can't make it authoritative. Whether it pleases us or not, what's accepted can also be rejected. In contrast, there's never a moment when traditional consciousness accepts or chooses its traditions—the traditions are the *starting point* of thought, beyond the realm of choice. The transformation of consciousness from the traditional to the modern variety is therefore irreversible. Whether we like it or not, we can't go home again.

Whether the trap-free life of traditional consciousness is happy or productive depends entirely upon the luck of the draw. If the external authority is benevolent and wise, its decisions will be good. But the authority may also be Hitler or the Reverend Jim Jones. The problem with traditional consciousness is that it leaves us no protection against Jim Joneses or—a far more frequent danger—those who would make our lives narrow and dull. For traditional consciousness is given up to authority without reservation. If we retain the option to reconsider our commitment in case things don't work out well, then we're only playing games with ourselves—the putative authority isn't an authority at all, however punctiliously we follow its dictates. In this case, ultimate authority remains in whatever self-generated criterion the external quasi-authority is to be judged by. Modern consciousness is only pretending to be traditional here. Except in rare circumstances, traditional consciousness is unalterable, for the advisability of any possible change is judged on the basis of the traditions themselves. If we could persuade biblical fundamentalists to entertain the question of the validity of the Bible, they would only seek the answer by looking it up in the Bible. We never get more than one chance to live traditionally. If the draw is unlucky—if the authority is self-serving, foolish, or mad—there is no turning back. We must follow it over the edge of the cliff.

In any case, for the modern mentality to which this book is addressed, traditional consciousness is no longer a live option. Absolute authority is finished for us. There's no one to push our buttons, keying planning, calculation, and prescription in and out as the occasion requires. And so we return to our dilemma: if we shut the prescriptive mode down even for a moment, allowing ourselves to run free, how will we get it switched on again when it's needed?

The intractability of this dilemma depends on an unconscious assumption. We've come upon unconscious assumptions before in our analysis of mental traps. But this one is the Primal Assumption upon which the entire structure of trapped modern consciousness is based. We suppose that impulse—the non-rational and non-prescriptive wellspring of action—is incapable of returning the reins to prescription on its own initiative; and that even if it could, it wouldn't know when it was appropriate to do so. That is, we assume that *only rational calculation can tell us when rational calculation is needed*. If this Primal Assumption is true, then we must indeed always keep the prescriptive apparatus running, always strive to stay on top of the situation, always be minding the store.

What would life be like if the Primal Assumption were false? It would mean that the urge to plan, calculate, and prescribe *arises impulsively*, like hunger and thirst, when the situation calls for it. It would also mean that we can stop planning, calculating, and prescribing when the need for these activities is over, for we would know that we'll spontaneously begin them again when it's useful to do so. Prescription would take its place *alongside* the other activities of life rather than being their *foundation*. We eat, we make love, we walk, we sleep—and sometimes we plan, calculate, and prescribe. In sum, we would cease to have mental traps. Modern consciousness would then have given way to *liberated consciousness*.

Is impulse capable of shouldering such a load of responsibility? Let's divide this question into two parts. First, once impulse rules, is it capable of returning the reins of action to prescription on its own initiative? Second, can it do so appropriately—is it capable of discerning when prescription is needed?

The first question is the easy one. Essentially we're asking whether we can impulsively begin to calculate and prescribe, or whether calculation and prescription must always come from prior calculation and prescription. The fact that almost all of us have at least some moments of impulsivity gives us our answer. If we are impulsive one moment and prescriptive the next, it can only be that prescription has arisen out of impulsivity. Our *starting* to make reasoned decisions can't be the result of a reasoned decision!

Can the spontaneous welling up of rationality be counted on to occur exactly when it's needed? Not infallibly. We can all remember circumstances in which we acted impulsively and things went worse for us than if we'd done a little figuring. We thoughtlessly encourage the attentions of a bore, and he importunes us for years afterward. Had we kept our prescriptive apparatus running, we might have foreseen this outcome and prescribed a more reserved demeanor for ourselves. But of course we make mistakes in the prescriptive mode as well. Our calculations are sometimes based on erroneous or incomplete information, and we sometimes misplace a decimal point or skip a step. We can't directly assess the relative efficacy of impulse and prescription by comparing the sum total of their outcomes—life is too complex. Nevertheless, it can be shown that there's no advantage to leaving the prescriptive mode running all the time.

The crucial point is that planning, calculating, and prescribing can function only on the basis of certain premises. When we decide (prescriptively) whether to be reserved or warm toward someone we've just met, we consider the likely outcome of both courses of action and choose the one that, everything considered, seems best. But what makes one outcome better than another? Why do we deem not having a relationship with someone better than having a boring relationship with him—or vice versa? Perhaps such a decision can be made to follow from some general principle such as "Do what gives you the most pleasure" or "Do whatever serves others best." But where do *these* general principles come from, in their turns? Perhaps from even more basic principles. But eventually the chain of rational justification has to stop at a principle or value that, from the viewpoint of rationality, is simply *given*. The deliberations of the prescriptive mode can't begin with a blank slate. The items it begins with—our most fundamental principles and values—must therefore come from impulse. We spontaneously, irrationally adopt them. There is no other way to start thinking.

It follows that the strategy of modern consciousness makes no sense. We leave prescription running all the time because of our lack of faith in impulse. Yet impulse lies at the very heart of our prescriptive activities. Every plan we make, every calculation, every reasoned decision begins with assumptions that were given to us by impulse. Thus our faith in rationality *presupposes* an even more fundamental faith in impulse. If the dictates of impulse are untrustworthy, then so are the products of rational deliberation. And if we trust rationality, then we are committed to trusting the impulse that gives birth to it. In either case, there's no advantage to be gained by the strategy of modern consciousness. Its only fruit is weariness.

This doesn't mean that it's always undesirable to deliberate or prescribe. The conclusion is rather that deliberation and prescription can be trusted to emerge on impulse when they're needed, just like breathing and blinking one's eyes. Therefore we can turn off the prescriptive apparatus without fear. We won't immediately dive over the edge of the nearest cliff. Of course, absolute security can't be guaranteed. It's always possible to break one's neck. But the habit of perpetually staying "on top" of every situation makes us work very hard for no return. In brief, it gets us into mental traps.

We are left with the question of what to do. We've already seen how every attempt to argue, command, insult, or otherwise persuade ourselves to desist from the useless mental work of one trap lands us immediately in another. The task of shutting down the prescriptive apparatus can't be accomplished by its continuing activity! The same dilemma confronts the insomniac striving mightily to fall asleep. The harder she works at it, the farther the goal recedes from her. For both sleep and liberated consciousness can be won only by the cessation of our prescriptive activity.

Indeed, falling asleep is always a little liberation—a victory of impulse over prescriptive control. A close analysis of how this familiar transition may be effected will tell us what we still need to know.

Sleep is unproblematic when we're certain that there is nothing at all we need to do about it. We simply go to bed, serene in the knowledge that sleep will come when our body requires it. If we try to cause it to come by our own efforts, we only keep it at bay by the noise of our mental activity. But if we have faith in our own organism, the goal is won without doing a thing. Our faith is a self-fulfilling prophecy. Similarly, in the liberated state of consciousness, the rational, prescriptive apparatus places its faith in the impulsive apparatus. Rationality performs whatever calculations it has been called upon to perform and then gracefully retires, serene in the knowledge that when its services are once again required, it will hear the summons.

This faith, of course, is more than an intellectual conviction. Indeed, we're assuming here that we've already been convinced of the desirability of liberation. We want to let go of the reins; we try to *prescribe* a policy of letting go; but we find that this maneuver is just a subtle way of hanging on. This condition also has its parallel in the realm of sleep. We're like an insomniac who has come to understand that she keeps herself awake by her own struggles. She knows that sleep will come as soon as she ceases to care about its coming. So she struggles to cease caring. What else is there to do?

In the case of insomnia, sleep does eventually come even to the most faithless. But it comes in a surprising way. The insomniac struggles, entirely in vain, to grasp sleep until she gives up from sheer exhaustion and despair. And then, precisely because she's given up, she falls asleep. The same process may also lead us from modern to liberated consciousness. We may prosecute the voluntary struggle to free ourselves to the bitter end. This paradoxical grasping at the state of letting go is bound to fail. Yet it may not prove entirely useless in the end. If we struggle with all our might, exhausting every possible stratagem of the rational, prescriptive apparatus, we may eventually reach so profound a level of despair that we simply give up the enterprise of pulling ourselves along by our own bootstraps. And then we're given the prize after all. For when we cease to prescribe, the administrative void is filled by impulse. The transition may take a while. At first we may lie around in a state of abject passivity, no longer knowing what to do. But when our bladder gets full, the task at hand will be clear enough.

"If a fool would proceed with his own folly, he will become wise." The shortcoming of this—the fool's—route to liberation is that we are extraordinarily hopeful and tenacious creatures. Great calamities—the irremediable failures of all our plans and dreams—may, if they don't destroy us utterly, result in liberation. But a lifetime of ordinary dissatisfaction is usually not long enough to make us give up.

We're ready to give the life of impulse a try. But because we aren't yet liberated, we can't let go of the reins, even on a trial basis. We want to escape from the prison of modern consciousness. But since we're *in* the prison, our actions *must* follow some regulative policy. We *must* stay on top of the situation. How then will we ever discover whether liberated consciousness really works?

The way out of this dilemma requires an exceedingly subtle maneuver on the part of rational consciousness. The trick is to adopt a regulative policy whose results are *identical* to the dictates of impulse. A concrete example will make this idea clear. The most elegant policy of the type we're looking for is the practice of *attentiveness*. We simply commit ourselves totally to paying careful attention to whatever we're doing. When we walk, we try to remain aware of every step; when we eat, we are attentive to the handling of knives and forks; and when we're angry or upset, we remember to watch ourselves being angry or upset. In this way, the compulsive need of the prescriptive apparatus to follow a definite line is entirely satisfied. We are always pursuing a clearly prescribed goal: to be fully attentive. But this goal doesn't determine the *content* of our activities. The policy of perfect attentiveness is compatible with our doing anything at all! With the prescriptive apparatus contentedly busy sustaining a policy of attention, impulse takes over by default. As in the case of liberation by despair, there may be an intermediate period of relative inactivity during which we don't know what to pay attention to. After all, our prescriptive policy fails to specify a concrete course of action. But we can fully count on our bladder to take us past this point of impasse.

The practice of continuous attention to the present permits us to satisfy our biological needs.

But can we live like this while leading a productive and creative life? If we intend only to watch ourselves, can we hold down a job, reform society, or raise a child? Our personal experiment will enable us to answer these questions for ourselves. By satisfying the presently felt imperative to follow a definite policy, the practice of attentiveness allows us to live impulsively on a trial basis. If everything goes well, we learn from direct experience that the store takes care of itself. When we're hungry, we eat; and when we need to calculate and make plans, the prescriptive apparatus is called in to calculate and make plans. In this way we acquire the faith necessary for making the transition to liberated consciousness. Once the transition is made, we can drop the project of attentiveness as well. It's only a crutch.

The faith required for liberation has nothing to do with arbitrary belief or wishful thinking. We've had a lot to say about the shortcomings of the rationalizing, calculating, and prescribing apparatus that rules modern consciousness. But modern consciousness can be transcended only when it cleaves unswervingly to its own truth. A glib pseudo-faith in the intrinsic goodness of inner impulses or outer saviors will not set us free. For modern consciousness, the only faith that counts for something is one that has withstood the test of relentless scrutiny with absolute intellectual honesty. Perhaps there is no salvation for us. Perhaps the fragile island of order and control so painstakingly won by our rationality is the only refuge. Perhaps life is ultimately absurd. It's possible for a *traditional* mind to achieve liberation without having to deal with issues like these. But there can be no transcendence of modern consciousness except by traversing the sea of nihilism. We won't be able to achieve inner peace until we're ready to face the possibility that conflict is unending. Let's not be comforted by hopes and lies. Let's dedicate ourselves wholly to the truth, wherever it may lead. For the rational mind to which this book is addressed, there is no higher master.

The Practice of Thought-Watching

appendix

The previous chapters have been devoted mainly to helping the reader detect and identify mental traps in everyday life. Unlike bird-watching, jogging, building a sailboat, or learning to speak a foreign language, this project makes no demand on our time whatever. The enterprise of trap identification slips easily into even the busiest schedule because it takes place *at the same time* as our other activities. We don't need to diminish the number of hours we put in at the office, or give up a moment's rest or recreation. In fact, it's our customary work and play that provides us with the arena for our investigations. Here is the perfect hobby! An overexclusive concern with high-fidelity audio equipment or golf may impoverish the rest of our life; but we can become mental-trap fanatics without narrowing the range of our interests, activities, and sympathies in the least.

There is, however, a special exercise that can hasten our progress. Of course, being in a hurry to get rid of traps is itself a trap. But when there's no pressing business or alluring pleasure over the horizon—when we have "time on our hands"—some of that time may profitably be devoted to the practice of *thought-watching*. The only equipment needed for thought-watching is a spot reasonably free of external distractions. The instructions couldn't be simpler: we sit quietly and watch our thoughts. That's all. In thought-watching, we don't try to think about anything in particular; but neither do we try to block or interfere with the thoughts that happen to arise. We just watch, as if at a movie.

Almost as soon as we begin this exercise, we learn an important lesson about the mind: *thoughts arise by themselves, even if we don't strive to will them into existence*. This truth can be deduced indirectly from our earlier discovery that thinking is often unconscious: obviously, we can't be willing our ideas into existence when we're unaware of them. But in thought-watching, we can observe in the full light of consciousness how thoughts come and go by themselves without the benefit of our assistance. To be sure, we *can* also exert a volitional influence on the stream of ideas. But the stream doesn't automatically dry up as soon as we cease to exert ourselves.

Thoughts continue to flow even when we stop pushing them into being from behind.

But this is only a preliminary observation. Sooner or later, every mental trap encountered in daily life also makes its appearance when we simply sit and watch our thoughts. And because we've temporarily suspended our competing interests, we are keener observers. Thought-watching is especially useful for learning to detect the momentary lapses into trapped thinking that are too fleeting to lay hold of in the heat of daily life. But thought-watching doesn't render the examination of daily life superfluous. It's only while we're immersed in the business of living that we commit the longer versions of each trap that consume us for hours, days, or even years at a time. Even here, however, the sensitization that results from thought-watching greatly improves the quality of our observations of daily life.

Fifteen or twenty minutes of thought-watching, practiced more or less daily, will quickly lead to some remarkable discoveries about our mental machinery. The novice thought-watcher will find, however, that thought-watching seems to be a difficult business. Actually, nothing could be easier. But at the beginning we spend very little of our thought-watching time actually watching our thoughts. Instead we try to *control* the flow of thought—to make it flow in one direction or another, or to suppress it altogether. Of course we can't simultaneously control our thoughts and just watch them emerge. The attempt to follow this contradictory program makes us increasingly tense. This is why the exercise appears to be difficult.

All this is just as it should be. For it's precisely at the moment when we leave off thought-watching and start to control that we fall into a trap. The traps don't simply pop into the range of our observing consciousness amidst other, non-traplike ideas. We *commit* them. So long as we're engaged in the enterprise of thought-watching, all intentional meddling with the flow of thought—mental "work" on any project whatever—is a trap. Strictly speaking, the traps don't come up *while* we're thought-watching, but rather when we cease to follow the instructions.

This isn't to say that we should never try to control our thoughts. On the contrary, exercises to improve our control were discussed in the chapter on division. But we also have to learn to *relinquish* control when it's appropriate to do so. If we've decided to watch our thoughts, control is useless by definition. *In this situation*, every attempt at control is a superfluous mental episode, i.e., a trap. This is what makes thought-watching so instructive: when no work at all is called for, we observe with great clarity the various ways in which we invent make-work for ourselves.

Let's see how the simplest trap, *persistence*, arises in the course of thought-watching. Having begun to watch, we may at first observe our ideas coming and going by themselves, just as the exercise requires. We're aware of the ticking of a clock. A scene from the past flashes before our eyes. Our nose itches. And that's that. Ideas of this kind arise and fall away without leaving a trace, "like birds flying across a cloudless sky." They're *self-contained* in the sense that they carry with them no requirement for further thinking. But it isn't long before we try to lasso one of our mental birds and use it for a mount. Having heard the ticking of a clock, we wonder what time it is; a scene from the past having flashed before us, we ask ourselves whether it really happened that way. And immediately we set to work on the problem. The project that grabs hold of us may be entirely inane—we think of Snow White and start to reconstruct the list of the seven dwarfs. At this time, the quality of our mental functioning changes completely. We are interfering in the flow of ideas with a definite purpose of our own. We're no longer thought-watching.

Of course, we can choose to find out what time it is, or reconstruct the past, or name the dwarfs *instead of* watching our thoughts. But let's assume that we don't really want to be counting dwarfs—that, in fact, we want to be thought-watching. Let's assume that it's entirely clear to us that we'll be none the worse for abandoning the dwarf project altogether. Nevertheless, having inadvertently begun the dwarf project, we find ourselves impelled to continue with it. Having thought of five of the dwarfs' names, it's hard for us to return to thought-watching until we come up with the missing two. That is to say, it's difficult not to *persist*. We had intended to sit down and just watch our thoughts; but instead we engage in a vigorous and pointed search through our stock of personal adjectives ending in *y*.

The topics we get stuck on when we are watching our thoughts are not uniformly pointless. Often we begin to think about issues that do have relevance to our life, but that can safely be postponed until after the thought-watching session is over. In this case, we fall into the trap of *anticipation*. We designate a period of time for doing nothing but watching our thoughts; we clear the mental boards of all outstanding and pressing business, satisfying ourselves that there's no issue in our life that would suffer from a quarter-hour's postponement; and then we start. But it isn't long before one of these future issues lays hold of our attention. We begin to think about the dinner plans that we will have to make before the day is out, or the momentous vocational decision that we'll have to face within the month, or the perfect holiday that we're going to take some day. It may be clear beyond a shadow of a doubt that we don't stand to benefit by taking up these issues *now*, in the middle of thought-watching, rather than fifteen minutes later. And yet we do it anyway.

In these examples of persistence and anticipation, the content of our trapped thinking is indistinguishable from what might occur in daily life. The only difference is that we're likelier to detect the trap because we aren't busy doing anything else. We're like naturalists sitting quietly behind a bush, field glasses in hand. If we wait patiently enough, all the traps of daily life will make their appearance. We will persist, anticipate, revert to past grievances, formulate attitudes toward issues that don't concern us, accelerate breathlessly toward conclusions for which there is no pressing need . . . In daily life, we can only cast a sideward glance at these fabulous beasts as we pass them by, for we're always on one mission or another. But when we're thought-watching, we can observe them at our leisure and fully relish their astonishing properties.

These denizens of daily life aren't the only creatures to be observed in thought-watching, however. They constitute only the first and most obvious circle of trapped thinking. Once we become aware of them, we usually initiate various maneuvers that are designed to banish them from our mind. *These attempts to extricate ourselves and return to thought-watching invariably result in subtler versions of each trap*. We end up traveling from one trap to another and back again, with no exit in sight. A sequence may begin with any of the familiar trapped ideas of daily life. For illustrative purposes, let's suppose that we sit down to watch our thoughts and catch ourselves persisting in the construction of a list of Snow White's dwarfs.

Once we realize that we've been persisting, we may complain of our failure to thought-watch properly: "I've messed it up again!" Of course, telling ourselves that we have messed it up does not undo the fact that we've messed it up, nor does it yet get us on the right track. By complaining about an event that is irretrievably finished, we only exchange our persistence for the trap of *reversion*. Instead of uselessly thinking about the dwarf list, we're now thinking uselessly about the fact that we've been thinking uselessly! And when we realize that our reversionary ideas still don't bring us back to thought-watching—that we mess it up again by thinking that we've messed it up—we may revert to the reversion: "I've messed it up!—and now I've messed it up again!" Now we're face-to-face with an awesome infinite regress in which each lamentation of a past failure gives us cause to lament again: "I've messed it up again—and again—and again . . . !" The only way out of the labyrinth is to drop the issue entirely—to permit one of our successive failures to pass without comment.

Alternatively (or additionally) we may try to

sustain thought-watching by perpetually reminding ourselves of what we're doing. We think:
"I'm thought-watching—just thought-watching—
nothing else." It's as though we were trying to
keep our incipient ideas about competing projects
at bay by calling out the name of what we want to
be doing. But *telling* ourselves that we're thought-
watching is not yet thought-watching. It's *formulation*. It's easy to fool ourselves, however. After a
few moments of high-quality thought-watching,
we may even say to ourselves, "*Now* I'm really
doing it!"—without realizing that we cease to be
really doing it as soon as we have that thought.
When we catch ourselves in this subtle variety of
formulation, we may once again take the first step
toward an infinite regress by thinking, "That's
formulation," as though naming the beast were the
same as vanquishing it. But of course naming the
formulation is just formulation over again: "That's
formulation—and so is that—and so is that . . ."

Regulation isn't very different from formulation here. Instead of trying to drown out the
intrusive dwarf project by invoking the name of
thought-watching, we legislate ourselves back to
our appointed task: "Get back to thought-
watching!" Of course, laying down the law that

we must thought-watch is still not the same thing as watching our thoughts; and if we remain busy pushing ourselves around for the entire session— "Just keep watching! Stop persisting! None of that! Just watch!"—we won't have watched our thoughts at all. Furthermore, when we come to appreciate the futility of regulating our thought-watching, we're apt to start making regulations against regulating. A typical sequence might go like this:

> Sneezy . . . Dopey . . . That's persistence.
> Stop persisting. Just watch thoughts. But
> that's regulation. Stop regulating. Just watch
> thoughts. But that's still regulation. Stop
> regulating . . .

How do we get out of a vicious circle of this kind? Nothing could be simpler: instead of *telling* ourselves to stop regulating and just watch thoughts, we need only stop regulating and just watch thoughts.

Another strategy for vanquishing intrusive projects is to tell ourselves that we will postpone their consideration until after the thought-watching session is over. But to decide *now*, when we already know what to do for the next quarter-hour, what we will do *next* is a *one-step anticipation*. We've already realized that it's unnecessary to complete the dwarf list at this time; but we don't yet see that it's equally unnecessary to decide, at this time, *when* we will complete it or whether we'll complete it at all. Here again we may suffer from a piling up of one trapped idea upon another. When we come to understand that "I'll do it after thought-watching" is anticipatory, we tell ourselves that we needn't decide now when to do it—that we will consider the problem of when to do it after thought-watching is over. But this idea commits again the very trap it wishes to disavow. We needn't decide now when to complete the dwarf list, *and* we needn't decide now when to decide.

After the dizzying spirals of reversion, formulation, regulation, and anticipation, it's refreshing to contemplate the simpleminded obtuseness that causes us to *accelerate* during thought-watching. As in the previous cases, we look in at the moment we catch ourselves persisting in the construction of a useless dwarf list. Wishing to get back to thought-watching, we may berate ourselves for our failure (reversion), tell ourselves what we are supposed to be doing (formulation), order our-selves back to work (regulation), or reschedule the intrusive project for a later time (anticipation)—all of which are as different from thought-watching as the original persistence was. Another strategy is to try to rush through the intrusive project as rap-idly as possible so that we may sooner return to thought-watching. That is, we add the trap of acceleration to our original persistence. Now we are not only thinking about the dwarf list. We are also thinking about the *end* of the dwarf project—about how desirable it is to reach the end, how close we are to the end, and so on. Our concern with finishing as quickly as possible is a *second* intrusive project that takes us even further away from the attitude of thought-watching. In addition to ideas like "Dopey" and "Isn't there one that starts with an *M*?" we're also thinking, "Only two more to go and I'll be done!"

Fixation is a marvelously subtle phenomenon of thought-watching. At first glance, it may even seem that the occasion of thought-watching is incompatible with its occurrence. Since we don't have a future goal in mind, what is there for us to wait for? What we often wait for in thought-watching is *the end of the thought-watching session.*

Instead of just watching our thoughts, we conceive of ourselves as engaged in a mental exercise having a certain duration. We think of getting through a session to the end as scoring a point in some private game. The result is that we have a project to keep us busy from beginning to end: finishing the session. Of course this particular project doesn't require us to *do* anything. The completion of the thought-watching session can't be expedited; it comes by itself. We are just like a host waiting for his guests to arrive, and we make the same mistake: we begin to mark time. We may actually keep track of how much time is left: "One more minute to go . . . thirty seconds . . ." Or we may sit in a state of suspension, not actually thinking *about* the end but mutely straining toward it nonetheless. In either case, we become so intent on *having* watched our thoughts that we forget all about watching them.

When someone calls us from downstairs while we are thought-watching, we may adamantly *resist* the interruption, telling ourselves that we're not going to stop our exercise for anything. We may even shout back with annoyance: "Don't bother me now. I'm watching my thoughts!" But we couldn't have such an idea unless we had already stopped watching our thoughts. Indeed, we quit watching as soon as we become aware of being interrupted. Had we abided in a purely observational attitude, the call from downstairs would have been no more than a sound, like the whistling of the wind. To experience it as an interruption means that we've already made it the first step of a new enterprise: getting the interruption off our back. There's no question of *continuing* to thought-watch, for thought-watching is already behind us. This is what sets resistance during thought-watching apart from the garden-variety resistances of everyday life: when we struggle to ward off interruptions to our thought-watching, we're trying to preserve something that has already ceased to exist.

Procrastination is nothing more than resistance to the new when we're not committed to any other definite enterprise. Thus it can't really occur *during* thought-watching itself. However, it's often observed before we start to thought-watch. Before we can settle down to our exercise, we feel the need to "clear the boards" of various outstanding obligations that might otherwise interrupt us. We check the rest of the day's schedule to make certain that nothing needs immediate attention, order

up the house, and review the fundamental principles and aims of our existence. The same sequence
of events might precede any new enterprise.
Because it occurs prior to an undertaking, procrastination is the only trap that doesn't reveal a new
face when we watch our thoughts.

Any extraneous topic taken up during
thought-watching may be *amplified* ad nauseam.
We catch ourselves anticipating what we're going
to say at an important interview tomorrow, and
we try to accelerate to the end of the task in order
to return to thought-watching. But the complete
and absolute end never seems to come. There's
always another possible question to find a reply
for. Even when the task is clearly finite, we
become uncertain about our earlier findings
before we reach the end, and then we have to
repeat. Having finally come up with the seventh
dwarf, we forget who the first one was and we
must start all over again.

All this, however, is garden-variety amplification. There's also an exotic variety rarely seen
outside the steamy environment of thought-
watching. We've noted again and again that the
very attempt to preserve thought-watching is
responsible for calling these exotic types into

being. The attempt to order ourselves back to thought-watching catapults us into regulation; the rescheduling of extraneous projects for a later time results in anticipation; and so on. Similarly, we fall into an amplification when we try to reason our way back to thought-watching. For example, we may point out to ourselves that we will suffer no disadvantage from dropping the extraneous project at this time. But we can't know this to be true without a review of all the potential disadvantages. Unfortunately, there's no end of potential disadvantages to consider. And even if we could establish this premise on unshakable grounds, it wouldn't yet be enough to permit the ironclad deduction that we should get back to thought-watching. For what if we simply enjoy working on the extraneous project? Well, we're not enjoying it. We're not enjoying it, and there are no disadvantages to dropping it—that seems to be the end of the matter. But what if there's another crucial consideration that presently escapes us? What if we've made a mistake in our reasoning? We had best review the argument from the start . . .

The last refinement of this line of thinking is reached when we realize that we have been amplifying. We then remind ourselves that amplification is a trap—but *is* it? We had best review the arguments showing that it's a trap, just to be sure. We try to escape from this new dilemma by reminding ourselves that we've *already* reviewed these arguments, indeed that we've done so when we were at our keenest, so that a reconsideration at this time is entirely superfluous. We *know* that amplification is a trap. But do we? What if our memory is in error?

Division is commonly the last of three successive errors of thought-watching. We fall into a first trap by inappropriately working on some mental project—for example, we persist in the construction of a dwarf list. We fall into a second trap by making a project out of remedying the situation—for example, we try to regulate ourselves back to thought-watching. And then we fall into the third trap of division by moving back and forth between the first two traps:

> Sneezy . . . Stop this nonsense! Dopey . . .
> Get back to thought-watching! Isn't there
> one that starts with an *M*? No more of this!

We would do better simply to finish the dwarf-list in peace.

Naturally, a division need not be limited to two traps. We can commit any number at one sitting. The reader may find it instructive to identify the successive traps fallen into in this representative monologue (the answers are given right after the monologue):

> Sneezy . . . Only two more names to go. But I haven't been thought-watching! I must get back to it. There's no need to work on this dwarf list. I can finish it after the session . . . There—*now* I'm doing it. Just a few minutes more . . .

After the original persistence of "Sneezy," these thoughts are instances, respectively, of acceleration, reversion, regulation, amplification, anticipation, formulation, and fixation. All of them together constitute a rather fierce but not at all unusual division. This is what it sounds like on the inside when we first sit down to watch our thoughts.

Everything we do to get back to thought-watching seems to land us in another trap. Yet the exit is in plain sight. There's nothing mysterious here. We're simply misled by our grammatical categories. We assume that "thought-watching" is something to do because it's a verb like "eating" or "making money," and we set out to do it right. This is like assuming that "Thursday" refers to a thing because it's a noun, and setting out in search of its precise geographical location. In fact, thought-watching isn't a project at all. It isn't a matter of doing, but of *ceasing* to do. Thought-watching is the condition we're in when, remaining wide awake, we no longer do anything. Thus we can't *do* thought-watching at all; we can only let it happen. If we try to stop an intrusive project by an act of some sort, then that act itself must inevitably become a second intrusive project. We get nowhere by cursing at ourselves, constructing good arguments, or laying down the law. The only remedy is to drop it—and *saying* "Drop it!" is not dropping it.

When we're thought-watching, we literally have nothing to do. Yet we manage to create a monumental round of chores and problems out of this nothing. Is it any wonder that we needlessly complicate our work when there *is* something to be done?

acknowledgements

Primary thanks go to a succession of teachers of the art of living: Lao Tse, Gautama Buddha, G. I. Gurdjieff, Carl Jung, Krishnamurti, Aldous Huxley, Philip Kapleau, Robert Aitken, Nechung Rinpoche, Ram Dass, and Kaila Kukla. For getting the book out there, however, I have to thank my agent, Robert Mackwood. What they say is true: you need a good agent. I tried and failed to get the attention of publishers for years before Robert came along and sold the book to two of them within a couple of weeks.

Having two simultaneous publishers—Doubleday in Canada and McGraw-Hill in the US—has been an interesting experience. For one thing, it seems that there are national differences in punctuation practices: one copy editor deleted most of my commas, while the other one nearly doubled their number. But the main consequence

243

of my dual literary citizenship has been that it brought me into contact with two of the most helpful and most pleasant people that I've ever worked with—my Canadian editor, Nick Massey-Garrison, and my American editor, Holly McGuire. Their enthusiasm and support have been unflagging. They've lavished my project with care as though it were their own. Holly sent me about a dozen e-mails on the precise wording of the subtitle; and Nick, who seems to have understood the book better than I have, made suggestions that led to major structural improvements. Thanks, Nick and Holly.

About the Author

André Kukla is Professor Emeritus at the
University of Toronto, and has taught in both
the Departments of Psychology and of Philosophy.
He has published numerous philosophical and
psychological articles and books, including books
by Oxford and MIT Press.